My Name Is Not 18121-018

ENDORSEMENTS

Similar to Sammie, I have had some challenging times along my journey and had to make choices and decisions that would shape my future. Sammie's journey and testimonials will give you insight into his growth and development as he put the pieces together in his life.

Warrick Dunn – Florida State University Hall of Fame, National Championship Winning Running Back / NFL great and First Round Pick by Tampa Bay

I have known Sammie for a long time and some of the trials he has endured and how he came out successful on the other side. I am excited about his story being available to everyone.

Charlie Ward - Heisman Trophy Winning Quarterback, National Champion at Florida State University, and NBA First Round Draft Pick By the New York Knicks

In the locker room, after winning the 2022 Cheez-It Bowl, I told the team they would not be remembered just because of a number. They will be remembered by the way they played, by their passion, their character, and by the love they have for each other. The same goes for individuals. Sammie was given a number by the Federal Bureau of Prisons, but his name was redeemed. Our Florida State Family doesn't just remember Sammie by his production on the field, but also by who he was and is as a person. Sammie and Tim have written a riveting must-read book about a life transformed by the saving power of Jesus Christ.

Mike Norvell – Head Football Coach, Florida State University

Tim and Sammie have written an incredible book about how the twists and turns of life don't define us, but it's what God says about us and who we are in Christ that matters most.

Dr. Tim Hill, General Overseer – Church of God,
speaker / author including *Furnace Grace*

I had the pleasure of getting to know and spend time with Sammie Smith during the seven years he served as the FCA Director of Character Development for the University of Mississippi football program. Sammie's life story and journey are truly inspiring and have had tremendous impact on athletes, coaches, and many others in his sphere. I encourage you to read his story and guarantee you will be blessed and encouraged.

Michael Ducker - Retired CEO FedEx Freight

If you like sports, you will love this book! The game of life can be tough sometimes. But God's playbook is always perfect. Thankfully, the final score in life is not summed up by one play, but rather our acceptance of Jesus Christ as our Savior and following His playbook.

Jason Crabb – Multi Grammy winning
Christian singer-songwriter

Sammie's story is a testament of how faith can change life's trajectory when we choose it. Turmoil doesn't have to define our path in motion.

Nelda Cales, Founder and President of Anchored in Motion,
EVP Atlantic Bay Mortgage Group

Sammie's story and his presence here at Ole Miss has been integral to the spiritual growth of our coaches and players. He has been an asset to our program. This book is a must read.

Coach Lane Kiffin - Head Coach, Ole Miss Rebels

As we read in Proverbs 22:1, a good name is rather to be chosen than great riches. In this quick and impactful read, Tim and Sammie have shared this truth in the story of Sammie's life. Although the Federal Bureau of Prisons assigned a number to Sammie, that number didn't define him. His name is Sammie Smith, not 18121-018. Because of his faith in Christ and work in ministry through the Fellowship of Christian Athletes, God is using Sammie and his story to have a positive impact on student athletes and many others across America.

> **Terry Bolton** - Lead Pastor, Sale Creek Church of God

I had the pleasure of bringing Sammie Smith to Ole Miss. His story of redemption is powerful and was impactful on our staff and players. This will be an encouraging read.

Coach Hugh Freeze – Head Football Coach, Auburn University

I was with Sammie for four years at the University of Mississippi. During that period, his devotional time with our coaches and pre-game chapels with our players was very influential in our spiritual growth as men. I always enjoyed the time my family and I had at our optional Sunday morning worship services. This book will be like having Sammie as your own personal Character Development Coach

> **Matt Luke** - Former Head Coach for the University
> of Mississippi and National Champion Offensive Line
> Coach for the University of Georgia

It is both an honor and a privilege to write this endorsement for Sammie Smith's book. It was my good fortune to have shared in the recruiting of one of FSU's greatest athletes and then, as Florida State's Head Track and Field Coach for Men to have personally been able to coach him for three years on the track. As a repeat conference champion Sammie always put his heart and his best effort into competition and his book, I'm sure, will reflect that same heartfelt determination.

Richard "Dick" Roberts - Head Track & Field Coach / Men - Florida State University - 1978-1988

I have known Sammie since he played junior high football and have witnessed his ups and downs both on the football field and off, but through all that, he has a story of redemption that everyone should know and read about through this book.

John Peery – Retired Editor, The Apopka (Fla.) Chief - weekly newspaper.

Everything we do should be on purpose and for a purpose. Sometimes, the twists and turns of life can throw all of us off course a bit. In this powerful book, Tim and Sammie share how Sammie's faith in Christ helped him get back on track and begin to minister to student athletes in a way to help them live their life as an overcomer. This is a must read and a great gift for anyone you know who wants to live life on a higher plane!

Tiffany Fisher - Founder of Close With Purpose, Producing Regional Manager – Supreme Lending

Sammie Smith burst into my consciousness with his record setting 288-yard performance against District Rival Lake Mary in the opening football game of the 1983 season; a debut that ultimately led to his selection as a Number 1 draft choice of the Miami Dolphins. Sammie's amazing life journey includes some of the best moments that life has to offer; his journey also includes some of the most painful experiences any person can endure in this world. In this book, Sammie shares his exceptional story in unsparing detail, the good, the bad and the heartbreaking. This book is riveting and powerful in its unsparing honesty and uplifting and inspiring as an example of the impact one man can have when he gives his life to Christ. Everyone--coach, ballplayer, or private citizen will find inspiration in these pages that can help them to live a better, more impactful, more meaningful life.

Roger Franklin Williams - Host "Talkin' Old School with Roger Franklin Williams" - On-Air Voice of Apopka Blue Darter Football FM 94.9/AM 950 Salem Media Group

Where do I start with all the memories of Sammie Smith & The Apopka High School football program? He came from a wonderful family I knew quite well; Sammie was one of the most heavily recruited high school football players in Florida history. His career at FSU & The Miami Dolphins is well documented. Today Sammie is a servant of our Lord and Savior Jesus Christ.

Don Chip Gierke - High School football & baseball coach for over 40 years in Florida.

I have known Sammie Smith for over 40 years. I recruited him out of Apopka, Florida to play football for us at Florida State University. He was the top high school football player in the state his senior year. While Sammie was a student athlete at FSU, he mentored our children while taking them fishing, as well as attending their little league ballgames. I have a great deal of confidence and faith in Sammie and trust him with everything. Over the years we have become very close friends. I have seen him navigate through the ups and downs of life. Sammie's playbook in life is his Bible, and faith is his source of success. I believe this book will impact many lives as Sammie is the epitome of courage and humility. Read it, enjoy it, and let it inspire you to live your life as an inspiration and role model for others.

Jim Gladden – FSU Associate Head Football Coach, Emeritus Outside Linebackers / Defensive Ends.

What is purpose? If defined, it means "the reason for why something is done, created or for which it exists." I choose to expand on that by including the meaning and the process of the term journey. We all begin the journey from the moment we are born. The challenge of purpose begins with maturity, and when an individual is truly ready to identify their purpose. In the last year, my journey and purpose are being defined for my desire to be closer to God and His purpose for us; and for His reason we were created and exist. As a leader throughout my career that has included many failures and triumphs, and now my journey to serve God, Sammie and Tim have been able to communicate a true-life story that will help readers assess their own lives and consider how to achieve more for themselves through our Savior Jesus Christ. I would highly recommend this book to all persons wanting to define their purpose and journey.

D. Bryan Parker - President – Mortgage Bankers Association of the Carolina's (MBAC) Vice President / Southeast Regional Manager – Monarch Mortgage, A Division of Blue Ridge Bank

Sammie is living the Game of Life at the highest level! We have been lifelong friends. This is a story of redemption through our Lord, Jesus Christ. Sammie's high and low experiences in each phase make a remarkable story and an inspiration of hope to many. This book is a true testament of what can happen when you turn your life over to the Lord. We are proud to call Sammie our friend.

Diane and Ed Brooks

I came to know Sammie Smith in 1985 when he was arguably the best high school player in Florida and I was a sportswriter covering recruiting for The Osceola, a newspaper devoted to Florida State University sports. Every college coveted the 6-2, 235-pound athlete who possessed elite sprinter's speed, so when Smith chose to commit to Bobby Bowden's Seminole program, it encouraged other top-rated Florida players to sign with the Seminoles too. Smith was the bell cow of the 1985 class, which was considered the best in FSU history and would later be credited with starting an NCAA Dynasty with 14 consecutive years of ten-win seasons and top five finishes. A mutual friend, Ed Brooks, introduced me to Sammie's mother and father. This provided early insight into the person inside the helmet. Sammie went through trials and tribulations in sports and later in life with his arrest, incarceration, and redemption.

Over the years, I wrote numerous stories about Sammie being knocked down, or knocking others down, only to get back up. But those heroic sports exploits were only a prelude to his greatest triumph. I encourage you to read this inspirational life story and to share this book with someone in need of a blessing.

Jerry Kutz – Publisher - The Osceola

In the NFL Draft, when it is announced that a team is On The Clock, it simply means that a final decision must be made by that team for the upcoming draft pick within the allotted time. What is not seen is the amount of preparation and work that has been done by the team, the athlete, and the agent to get to that point in the process. It's the same in life and business. We may measure success by key variables, but there is always more going on behind the scenes. That's where the level of success, or lack thereof, is determined. In this book, Tim and Sammie take you behind the scenes in Sammie's life and share with you the foundation of twelve pre-game chapels Sammie taught during the 2022 football season. Each one teaches important lessons that can help you be even more successful in life and business.

Bruce Tollner – NFL Super-Agent / Speaker / *New York Times* Bestselling Author of *On The Clock*

Sammie and I have served in ministry together since 2010! As an eyewitness to Sammie's story of triumph, trial, and redemption, I am excited to know that others can now get a glimpse behind the scenes and be as blessed by reading his story.

Wave Robinson – MBA, Former Regional Director with the Fellowship of Christian Athletes, Senior Pastor at Ultimate Ministries and Founder of Kingdom Financial Solutions

Sammie and Tim's compelling narrative explores the transformative power of God's love amidst life's mistakes, rebellion, and disobedience, offering a profound journey of redemption. With a captivating portrayal of personal growth, this book emphasizes the significance and reminder that it's God's power that causes real change in our lives. Through their transparent storytelling, readers are reminded that true victory transcends conventional measures, extending beyond the confines of any scoreboard.

Kevin Harrison – Uncommon Influence Coaching Founder and CEO

Sammie has a terrific story of early success followed by trials, tribulation, and then even greater success in what matters most. He is well respected within the Ole Miss family and the Oxford community. His time with the Ole Miss football program was positive and impactful. I believe this book by Sammie and Tim, written around Sammie's story and topics from pre-game chapels he taught the team during the 2022 football season, can impact your life in a positive way. I encourage you to read it and consider how your own story can be even better.

David Johnson - Recruiting Analyst and Publisher 247 Sports, Inside the Rebels

In today's world, people are constantly in search of identity and there's no shortage of ways that culture offers to both define us and allow us to define ourselves. Sammie and Tim have chronicled a captivating story of how Sammie went from being defined as an athlete, then an inmate. In the Lord's goodness and mercy, this journey led to Sammie finding his identity in Christ, the one who is unchanging and where we can all be anchored in the hope of knowing who we are in Him.

Kyle Sims, Founding Partner 49 Financial

MY NAME IS NOT
18121-018

MY NUMBER WAS GIVEN...
BUT MY NAME WAS REDEEMED

SAMMIE SMITH
WITH *NEW YORK TIMES* BESTSELLING AUTHOR TIM ENOCHS

NEW YORK

LONDON • NASHVILLE • MELBOURNE • VANCOUVER

My Name Is Not 18121-018
My Number Was Given...But My Name Was Redeemed

Published in New York, New York, by Morgan James Publishing. Morgan James is a trademark of Morgan James, LLC. www.MorganJamesPublishing.com

Proudly distributed by Publishers Group West®

Morgan James BOGO™

A **FREE** ebook edition is available for you or a friend with the purchase of this print book.

_____

CLEARLY SIGN YOUR NAME ABOVE

Instructions to claim your free ebook edition:
1. Visit MorganJamesBOGO.com
2. Sign your name CLEARLY in the space above
3. Complete the form and submit a photo of this entire page
4. You or your friend can download the ebook to your preferred device

ISBN 9781636983639 paperback
ISBN 9781636983646 ebook
Library of Congress Control Number:
2023949282

Cover and Interior Design by:
Chris Treccani
www.3dogcreative.net

Cover Photo Credit:
Ryals Lee Jr.

Interior Track Photo Credit:
FSU

Morgan James PUBLISHING

Builds

with...

Habitat for Humanity®
Peninsula and Greater Williamsburg

Morgan James is a proud partner of Habitat for Humanity Peninsula and Greater Williamsburg. Partners in building since 2006.

Get involved today! Visit: www.morgan-james-publishing.com/giving-back

In loving memory of my Father Sammie Lee Smith Sr, and my Son Jerrod Jamelle Smith, I hold on to the hope of seeing you both again in heaven. 1 Thessalonians 4:13-18.

To support my Ministry with the Fellowship of Christian Athletes visit https://my.fca.org/sammielsmith

Scan to support Sammie Smith

TABLE OF CONTENTS

Foreword   *xxi*

Chapter 1   My Name Is Not 18121-018   1
Chapter 2   Life Just Isn't Fair Sometimes   9
Chapter 3   Just Another Ordinary Day…Until   17
Chapter 4   Can't Shake It   25
Chapter 5   Prime Time In The Shadow   31
Chapter 6   Family, Friends, the Lord, and Time   37

Section Two   Contender vs. Pretender, FCA Chapels
               Ole Miss Football 2022 - Games 1-12   47
Game 1 :   Pride   49
Game 2:   Passionate & Patient / Passive Procrastinator   55
Game 3:   Challenges   61
Game 4:   Faith   67
Game 5:   Significance   73
Game 6:   Resilience   79
Game 7:   All In   85
Game 8:   A Certain Peace   93
Game 9:   Believe   99
Game 10:   Always Growing   105
Game 11:   Press Forward   111
Game 12:   Grateful   117

About the Author   123

FOREWORD

Dale Clayton
Vice President | Nations of Coaches

Sammie Smith and I both grew up in Central Florida. Our neighboring towns are north of Orlando, only 5 miles apart. Although I'm 20 years older, I knew of Sammie and his athletic accomplishments. We both were college athletes and played for committed Christian coaches who shared their faith with their staff and players. His coach was Bobby Bowden, and my coach was Phil Worrell. Fast forward to today… We are both believers in Jesus, and God has called each of us to full-time Sports Ministry. Sammie is on staff with the Fellowship of Christian Athletes, and I minister to college basketball coaches.

My name Is Not Number 18121-018 is a winner! Through the stories in this book, you will experience the result of a life changed by God for the Glory of God. Sammie's story is a reminder that man's true identity is not defined by what man calls him, but by who he is in Christ. When God changes your heart, you become a new person. Your life has new meaning and your desires and purposes change. Sammie, the star athlete, has become Sammie, the influencer of coaches and athletes. His desire now is to be a "Fisher of Men" Matthew 4:19.

Sammie's heart for those he serves is evident. You will enjoy the pregame and chapel talks he uses as tools, as well as many other nuggets found inside this book. I'm so grateful for Sammie and the way he's impacting the Kingdom of God. May we all drop the man-made labels we're given and live up to who God has called us to be.

CHAPTER 1

My Name Is Not
18121-018

A good name is to be chosen rather than great riches...

PROVERBS 22:1 NKJV

W ho are you?

Why are you here?

Not why are you here, wherever you are, reading this page.

There is a much more important question.

Why are you here on earth? Why are you who you are?

That brings us to another very important question… Who are you?

On October 13, 1992, on a stage at Georgia Tech in Atlanta, three men stood at podiums about to engage in a debate for the nation to consider who would be the best person to be Vice President of the United States of America. One of those men was Ross Perot's running-mate Admiral James Bond Stockdale. You read that right, "James Bond" Stockdale. He wasn't a movie hero. He was a national hero.

At the beginning of the debate, Admiral Stockdale brought up a topic that may have cost him the debate. However, it is a question we should all be asking ourselves every day.

His first words in the debate were:

Who am I?

Why am I here?

If addressed, the answers to those questions become the centerpiece of every decision in life.

If ignored, we just drift through life without ever living up to our potential.

This is my story.

In high school I played football and ran track. I was fast, strong, and loved the game. By my senior year, recruiting services rated me as the #1 high school football recruit in the nation.

But that didn't define me.

I could have played college football anywhere in the nation. I chose to be a Florida State Seminole and enjoyed success on and off the field playing for one of the greatest coaches of all time, Bobby Bowden.

But that didn't define me.

In the 1989 NFL Draft, I was selected by the Miami Dolphins as the 9th pick in the first round. Many people introduce me as a first round NFL draft pick.

But that doesn't define me.

While playing in the NFL, I was able to gain 1,881 yards, with an average of 3.5 yards per carry and was able to score 16 touchdowns.

But that doesn't define me.

I started a business building homes for people who needed assistance with getting a loan. I helped them through the process, even holding the mortgage myself when needed.

But that didn't define me... do you see where this is going? I didn't; at least not at first.

On September 11, 1995, I was arrested. In an Orlando Sentinel newspaper article written by Jim Leusner and published on September 15, 1995, I was referred to as:

> Former NFL football star Sammie Smith, Zellwood's home-town hero and anti-drug crusader, was accused Friday of being a major Central Florida crack cocaine supplier.

You see, that didn't define me either. But I was guilty and had to face the consequences and accept my responsibility.

The day of the arrest, I was traveling on Terrel Road – U.S. Highway 441 in Tangerine, Florida on my way to meet a group I was involved with concerning illegal actions. I noticed what I believed to be an undercover law enforcement vehicle in the vicinity and passed by the meeting point hoping to avoid an arrest. That plan didn't work out the way I had hoped. I found myself surrounded by several county Sheriff cars, along with an undercover car or two. My first thought wasn't to run. My first thought was... *I'm in trouble.*

My wife, daughter, and parents learned about my arrest on television.

It was a hard day that God used to transform my life.

Transformation came in steps, just as the judicial process came in steps.

Just as the first thought I had was... *I'm in trouble...* I was in trouble.

The way I slipped into trouble didn't matter… I was in trouble.

The good deeds I had done before and the good reputation I had in the community didn't matter… I was in trouble.

The accolades I had been given before were all still true… but I was still in trouble.

But there was good news.

As Dallas Holm would sing… although I had stepped out of God's will, I was never out of His care. It didn't matter where I was or what I was doing, God saw me. He knew exactly what was going on, and He cared.

He cared that I was doing something totally out of character.

He cared that I was doing something completely illegal.

He cared that I was doing something detrimental to myself and ultimately to others.

He cared for me, and He cares for you. No matter where you are, what you are going through, or what you are doing, He cares.

He cared enough to let me get arrested.

He cared enough to allow me to go to prison.

It was a time for me to accept responsibility for my actions. I had two debts to pay. One to society for my unlawful activity, and one to God for my sin. The debt to society was a sentence of 7 years in prison and a $10,000 fine. I paid my debt to society and earned an early release. The sin, well that was a different story. I was unable to pay that debt on my own. But thank God, Jesus paid that debt for me, and He did the same for you. It's just up to you to accept His offer.

Jesus did the hard work in paying my sin debt and He was there in prison helping me every step of the way as I paid my debt to society.

Somebody once said *real men don't cry*. I am a real man, but during that first night being locked in a cell, I cried. No longer did

I have a nice place to live with a 700 sq ft bathroom… my toilet was just another fixture in my new bedroom. My new bed wasn't like my comfortable bed at home, and I didn't have the freedom to do what I wanted to do and go where I wanted to go when I wanted. As bad as all that was, what I missed most was my family. I couldn't go home to them every night or wake up and see them every morning. I couldn't see them or talk to them when I wanted, or even when they needed me. My life was changed. That statement has a double meaning. Sure, my life had changed because I was locked up with a prison sentence I couldn't walk away from. It was also being changed because God was working in me to form a new man with a new life.

The night before I was to be moved from the local jail to prison, my dad shared something with me that I will never forget. He shared something I believe God gave him to share with me that would change my life forever. He said: *Sammie, don't leave here how you came.*

I knew exactly what he meant. He was telling me to allow God to work in my life to change me so that the man who walks out one day is not the same as the one who was about to walk in.

His words would resonate with me throughout the time I served.

It was the beginning of the process that transformed my life. Over six years later, I walked out a different man. I walked out a better man. I walked out a man driven by purpose and passion to help others.

God changed my life and gave me a new identity.

You see, when I was playing at Florida State, I wore my #33 jersey with my name on the back with a sense of pride and focus on the game. With the Dolphins in Miami, I wore different team colors, but had that same #33 with S. Smith on the back.

Prison was different. I was given a new uniform to wear. This time, I wasn't offered #33. I was assigned a number that would be my uniform number for the next six years.

My number was 18121-018.

But my name is not 18121-018.

My name is Sammie Lee Smith.

I am not defined as #33, or #18121-018, or even by the old Sammie Smith.

I am defined by who God says I am.

I am a new man in Christ Jesus. The old has passed away and the new has begun.

> This means that anyone who belongs to Christ has become a new person. The old life is gone; a new life has begun!
> **2 Cor 5:17 NLT**

As we journey together through the pages of this book, I will share with you screenshots of times in my life, some happy and some challenging. There have been times when I felt on top of the world and times when I felt the weight of the world on my shoulders. Walk with me through those times and I will show you how in every high and low God was with me every step of the way. He will be with you too!

You are not defined by your past, your present, or what others believe your future to be.

You are defined by who God says you can be and what His plans are for your life.

Like me, God can help you rewrite your story and change the narrative of your life.

Submit to Him and enjoy the journey!

Remember, God has great plans for you. He has plans you can't even imagine!

Let's go!

Reflection Questions:

1. What do you believe people think when they hear your name?

2. What do you want them to think?

3. Is there a gap between what you believe they may think today and what you want them to think?

4. If there is a gap, what 2-3 things can you do today to close that gap?

5. What else do you need to Keep, Start, or Stop doing to have the name you want?

6. What is your prayer concerning this chapter?

7. Is your purpose in life crystal clear? If not, see the Irrefutable Success University page and QR code on page 123 in this book for more information and a free month of Irrefutable Success University.

CHAPTER 2

Life Just Isn't Fair Sometimes

*...he took Joseph and threw him into the prison
where the king's prisoners were held,
and there he remained.*
GENESIS 39:20 NLT

The date was November 29, 1986. It was a rainy night in Tallahassee, Florida. The temperature was between 64-68 degrees, and the wind was blowing out of the southeast at 7-10 miles per hour. It wasn't exactly a picture-perfect night for football. However, Doak Campbell Stadium was rocking! Seminole Nation turned out in a big way to watch us play the Florida Gators. There were 62,307 fans there braving the elements to watch the game. Florida had won the last five games against us, and we were primed to stop that streak.

As a pre-game tradition at Florida State and in partnership with the Seminole Tribe of Florida, Chief Osceola rides Renegade, Florida State's beautiful white horse, onto the field to plant the flaming spear at midfield. The *War* Chant was not dampened by the rain, neither was the *Tomahawk Chop*. This was our home game, and we were set for the game to begin.

Florida received the opening kickoff. I was on the sideline, focused and ready to have a productive night despite the rain. By the time that rain-soaked game ended, I had a net gain of 116 yards and a touchdown. Well, that was the official count. Officially, we lost the game 17-13. But there is a back story. Hidden on the 18th line of the third page of the *NCAA Official Scoring Summary* is a little stat that impacted the outcome of the game.

Down by four points, my number was called for a play I will never forget. It was a play that didn't count in my personal stats for the game. Yet, it is one of the few plays in the rich history of Florida State Seminole football that has its own name.

I got the ball from Danny McManus, saw a crease, and hit it. I was off to the races. Only wet grass on 52 yards of a muddy field stood between me and a touchdown that would have won the game for us. I crossed the goal line and was ready to celebrate. Yet, that isn't the touchdown I have credit for in the official record book for that game. Those 52 yards are not part of the 116 yards beside my name. Concerning my official stats and final score of the game, that play never happened.

So, what is on the 18th line of the third page of the NCAA Official Scoring Summary?

The third page is titled: *NCAA FINAL TEAM STATISTICS*.

The 18th line is: *PENALITIES NUMBER – YARDS*.

The numbers listed are simple: *15 - 116*.

That's it… 15 - 116. It means we had 15 penalties for 116 yards.

I had crossed the goal line for what I thought to be a go-ahead touchdown. Rather than looking back to see team members rushing to celebrate our score and seeing fans celebrating in the stands,

I saw the vast majority of the 62,307 fans at the game weren't celebrating. They were stunned. No one on my team was on their way to the endzone to celebrate with me. They were on their way back to the line of scrimmage. What happened?

I knew I hadn't stepped out of bounds, and nobody was off-sides. There was no way there was a holding call because it had happened so fast. I was gone and there was no reason to even think about a holding call. But that's exactly what was called. There was a flag laying on the field. When the flag was picked up and the penalty was announced, they called holding on our receiver, Herb Gainer. But nobody blames Herb.

That play is known in Florida State football history as the *Phantom Hold*. I don't know of a single person at the game or who was watching on TV who saw Herb Gainer hold anyone on that play. All I know is that the flag was thrown, the official made the call, my touchdown didn't count, and we officially lost the game. I also knew that we had to accept it… fair or not. Once the call was made, there was no mechanism to take it back. We just had to line up again and run another play.

In the first chapter, I shared with you details of a very difficult time in my life. During that time, I accepted responsibility for my actions. While we all need to accept responsibility for our own actions, there are also times in life when we must accept things that are not fair. Decisions and actions of other people can adversely affect our lives. While I don't have to accept responsibility for the actions of other people, there are times I must accept the result from actions taken by other people. Sometimes, life just isn't fair.

The book of Genesis, in the Bible, is not just a book about creation. One of the great stories in Genesis reveals how a man named Joseph was treated unfairly. At first, he was treated unfairly by his own brothers who sold him as a slave. That wasn't fair! In fact, it was morally wrong. But Joseph didn't have a choice. Let me rephrase that… Joseph didn't have a choice whether to be sold by his brothers, but he did have a choice how he reacted to it. He chose to react by being excellent in all he did. He chose to be a winner.

As the story goes, he chose to be excellent in all he did, and God gave him favor. After a while, Potiphar (the captain of the guard for Pharaoh, the King of Egypt) promoted Joseph to be his personal attendant and run his house. Joseph was put in charge over everything Potiphar owned. Once again, something very unfair happened to Joseph.

As he was simply going about his work focused on excellence in his position, Potiphar's wife noticed Joseph and tried to get him to sleep with her. But Joseph was committed to excellence in everything he did, including serving Potiphar and not having an affair with Potiphar's wife. The problem was that she wouldn't give up.

Here's how it went down in Genesis 39:10-23 (NLT)

> *¹⁰ She kept putting pressure on Joseph day after day, but he refused to sleep with her, and he kept out of her way as much as possible. ¹¹ One day, however, no one else was around when he went in to do his work. ¹² She came and grabbed him by his cloak, demanding, "Come on, sleep with me!" Joseph tore himself away, but he left his cloak in her hand as he ran from the house.*

> *¹³ When she saw that she was holding his cloak and he had fled, ¹⁴ she called out to her servants. Soon all the men came running. "Look!" she said. "My husband has brought this Hebrew slave here to make fools of us! He came into*

my room to rape me, but I screamed. ¹⁵ *When he heard me scream, he ran outside and got away, but he left his cloak behind with me."*

¹⁶ *She kept the cloak with her until her husband came home.* ¹⁷ *Then she told him her story. "That Hebrew slave you've brought into our house tried to come in and fool around with me," she said.* ¹⁸ *"But when I screamed, he ran outside, leaving his cloak with me!"*

¹⁹ *Potiphar was furious when he heard his wife's story about how Joseph had treated her.* ²⁰ *So he took Joseph and threw him into the prison where the king's prisoners were held, and there he remained.*

Not fair! Right?

Once again, Joseph had a choice. Just as before, he chose excellence and became the leader of all the prisoners until the day he was released. After that, God used him to work out His plan to save the nation. What a turnaround!

The real story here is that no matter what happened to Joseph, fair or unfair, he continued to pursue excellence in all he did…

²¹ *But the Lord was with Joseph in the prison and showed him his faithful love. And the Lord made Joseph a favorite with the prison warden.* ²² *Before long, the warden put Joseph in charge of all the other prisoners and over everything that happened in the prison.* ²³ *The warden had no more worries, because Joseph took care of everything. The Lord was with him and caused everything he did to succeed.*

We've all had to face things in life that just wasn't fair.

Of course, I wasn't happy when I saw that penalty flag for holding. What made things worse is that even today, no one saw anything to support the holding call. Still today, that play is called the *Phantom Hold*. Whatever the ref thought he saw, no one else saw it. From all other accounts, there wasn't a hold by Herb Gainer on that play. But the only account that mattered was that of the ref who called it holding.

How we respond to those unfair moments can make us or break us. They can also help us know how to respond the next time something unfair happens. I could have walked off the field that night and said football isn't fair... I quit. Had I done that, I would have never played out the rest of my time at Florida State and would have never been drafted as the 9th overall pick in the 1989 NFL Draft.

You see, that wasn't the first, or the last time I have faced something that was unfair as it relates to football...

In the 1989 Sugar Bowl, we played Auburn.

After a 69-yard run for a touchdown, I turned around to see that play was being called back because of a holding penalty. Thankfully, we won that game. But I didn't get to count those yards, or the touchdown. I had done nothing wrong but had to accept the consequences of a rule violation.

Prior to that, in my junior year in high school, we had a great team. We had 3 All-Americans and one runner-up on our team. From that team, 9 teammates went on to play at the D1 Level (the highest) in college football. We were in the playoffs in a close game with Winter Park, a powerhouse football program in the state that year. We would have won the game, but after our receiver had missed a catch, the ref thought he had caught it and fumbled it. It stopped what might have been a game winning drive. We could all see it clearly from where we were on our sidelines and knew the ref just had a bad angle and made a bad call.

It didn't matter. When the game ended, we had lost. We had to accept what was called. We walked off the field knowing our season was over, but not our career in football.

We all must live one moment at a time, and some things we experience in those moments just aren't fair. But that's how we get from one minute or one year in life to the next… we live in the moment, but we don't have to be overcome by the moment. The moment doesn't own us. Something unfair may affect us in a moment, but it doesn't own us. We should own it. Our reaction is our choice.

Let it be what it is, a moment… just a moment. Learn from it, react to it in a spirit of excellence. Like Joseph, we don't have to like it, but we can move on with a winning strategy. Don't be controlled by the emotions of the moment. Own the emotions. Own the moment! Be the champion you were created to be… and handle it like a pro knowing you've got this! Moments, good or bad, don't last… champions do! Be a champion!

Reflection Questions

1. Have you ever thought life just isn't fair (for yourself or others)?

2. If so, describe that feeling and the circumstances that caused it to be that way.

3. What is the best thing to do when you believe you have been treated unfairly?

4. How should you best deal with memories of unfair treatment?

5. Have you ever treated someone unfairly (intentionally or unintentionally)?

6. If so, would it be good to ask for forgiveness or at least have a conversation with that person or those people?

7. What is your prayer concerning this chapter?

CHAPTER 3

Just Another Ordinary Day...Until

My enemies surround me like a pack of dogs...
PSALM 22:16(A) (NLT)

It was just another ordinary day. Like many mornings, I had decided to get some exercise done by taking a walk around my neighborhood. Oxford, Mississippi is a beautiful college town nestled in the foothills of north Mississippi. I was looking forward to an enjoyable walk. It was a beautiful day, and I was laced up and ready to go.

Of course, like everyone else, I had things on my mind. Like most days, I was thinking about how I could best serve my family and our team that day. I love what I get to do. My wife and I are involved with Fellowship of Christian Athletes at the University of Mississippi, the school where I earned my undergraduate degree, and we get to interact with some amazing student athletes who are developing into outstanding young men and women. I was already involved in the process of writing this book and had been thinking about all I wanted to share with you and how I wanted to share it. I was also thinking about an upcoming surgery I needed to have on my shoulder. Although I wasn't looking forward to that, I knew it needed to be done. Like you, life was happening, and I had a lot swirling around inside my mind. I just had no idea what was about to happen.

As I was walking, I was thinking about all things pertaining to life and was happy to be able to get out on a beautiful day to get some exercise. Like any walk around any neighborhood, I noticed the houses and lawns along the way. Of course, some were manicured, some were freshly cut, and some were probably ready to be cut that day. Some houses had been meticulously maintained, and some could use a little extra TLC. Like I said, it was just another ordinary day, and I was on an ordinary walk around my neighborhood.

I was alerted to unusually aggressive barking by a neighbor's dogs. It wasn't the yip-yip you might hear from small dogs. No, what I heard was coming from dogs big enough to cause concern. At first glance, all seemed well. My neighbor's daughter seemed to have the dogs controlled, and on a leash… until she didn't. When I saw separation (or green grass) between the girl holding the leash and the dogs, I knew I had a situation that would demand my full attention. No longer was it just wave, acknowledge the dogs, and walk on. These dogs were headed toward me on a mission. I knew I could be in for a serious confrontation.

I had their full attention, and they had mine.

Suddenly, everything swirling around inside my mind stopped. When I say stopped, I mean every thought I had, except for one, disappeared like a vapor. I had one thought left. Survive!

You may have heard the term fight-or-flight response. Some have called it the fight-flight-or freeze response. That just describes the normal psychological reaction that happens when one is threatened or perceives a threat. For me that day, there was no perceiving a threat. I saw two big dogs in a full-blown sprint coming my way. It's amazing how quickly you can think when you are focused and on full alert. Although I had been very fast when I played football, I wasn't as fast as I was before. Even then, I couldn't outrun a big dog. My two legs couldn't out pace their four. There was nowhere to go and nowhere to hide. Flight was out of the question. I decided it would be best to freeze first (to see what they would do) and be ready to fight.

I didn't start out that day to kick my neighbor's dog. But now, I had to be ready to defend myself. My hopes of them possibly seeing something beyond me they were racing toward quickly faded when it was confirmed... they were after me and I had to defend myself. I couldn't just stand there and let them chew on my leg. So, I did what I could to defend myself.

Maybe I could have successfully defended myself against one dog, but not two. As I was trying to deflect their attack and get them to stop any way I could, I lost my footing and fell. Yes, I fell. Now, I was lying on the ground almost completely defenseless, with two very aggressive dogs ready to tear into me.

I had tried to catch myself with my hand on the opposite side from the shoulder needing surgery. The good news is that I didn't cause further damage to my already injured shoulder. But in the process, I broke my forearm. I didn't just crack a bone in my forearm, it broke! I had also dislocated my wrist in the fall. At that point, I couldn't use my arms and hands to protect myself and I was much more vulnerable lying on the ground. To use a fighting term, I didn't have a puncher's chance. I couldn't punch.

Isn't life that way sometimes? We've all had times when we believe we've done everything we could to protect ourselves or others, and nothing worked. As we read the words of Psalm 22:16, our enemies surround us like a pack of dogs. I could add, and we are lying on the ground without having a puncher's chance.

Have you ever felt that way? Maybe you did everything you could to bring about good in a situation, but you still feel surrounded by enemies. Maybe the enemies are people. At times the enemies aren't people at all. There are times we are attacked by spiritual forces of evil trying to take us down… and keep us down.

There are times when we all feel defeated.

Maybe you feel the best you could do just wasn't good enough. That's how I felt lying on the ground with two vicious dogs growling at me. We all joke about something smelling like dog breath, but trust me, you don't want to be close enough to smell the breath of an attack dog. At that point, the smell of their breath is your least concern. I am a strong guy, and I had done everything in my power I knew to do and still found myself on the ground.

When that happens, it's good to go back to these verses of Psalm 22…

> *12 My enemies surround me like a herd of bulls;*
>   *fierce bulls of Bashan have hemmed me in!*
> *13 Like lions they open their jaws against me,*
>   *roaring and tearing into their prey.*
> *14 My life is poured out like water,*
>   *and all my bones are out of joint.*
> *My heart is like wax,*
>   *melting within me.*
> *15 My strength has dried up like sunbaked clay.*
>   *My tongue sticks to the roof of my mouth.*
>   *You have laid me in the dust and left me for dead.*
> *16 My enemies surround me like a pack of dogs;*
>   *an evil gang closes in on me.*

They have pierced[a] my hands and feet.
17 I can count all my bones.
  My enemies stare at me and gloat.
18 They divide my garments among themselves
  and throw dice[b] for my clothing.

19 O Lord, do not stay far away!
  You are my strength; come quickly to my aid!
20 Save me from the sword;
  spare my precious life from these dogs.
21 Snatch me from the lion's jaws
  and from the horns of these wild oxen.

22 I will proclaim your name to my brothers and sisters.[c]
  I will praise you among your assembled people.

PSALM 22:12-22 NLT

Thankfully, help is only a prayer away.

God is my strength, and He came quickly to my aid.

He spared my precious life from those dogs.

So today, in this chapter, I am proclaiming His name to my brothers and sisters.

I don't know what those dogs saw that day. Something stopped their attack.

I believe it was Someone (Someone bigger than you and me) stopped their attack.

Did God send an angel?

Did He just change their minds? I don't know.

All I know is that they didn't come at me when I was on the ground.

They still sounded aggressive, but they didn't attack again.

Once I was able to get up and get away from that situation, I needed medical attention.

I needed to delay the rotator cuff surgery I thought would be next so I could have surgery on my broken forearm. After that, there was rehab. But I am here to tell the story.

Here's what I told someone in a text the next day.

The enemy was trying to stop me from being effective.
But he will NOT win!

And he won't win with you either!

No matter what your circumstance is, do everything God has given you the ability to do to win, and trust in Him for the rest. With Him, there is no giving up!

With Him, there is no losing!

It was just another ordinary day because the enemy tries to attack every day.

In 2 Cor 4, we find:

[7] We now have this light shining in our hearts, but we ourselves are like fragile clay jars containing this great treasure. This makes it clear that our great power is from God, not from ourselves.

[8] We are pressed on every side by troubles, but we are not crushed. We are perplexed, but not driven to despair.

[9] We are hunted down, but never abandoned by God. We get knocked down, but we are not destroyed. [10] Through suffering, our bodies continue to share in the death of Jesus so

that the life of Jesus may also be seen in our bodies. - 2 Cor. 4:7-10 NLT

It was just another ordinary day... until He came to my rescue!

REFLECTION QUESTIONS

1. Have you ever felt you have been under a direct attack by a person or a group of people? (this goes beyond being treated unfairly)

2. Is there anyone or group it would be good for you to forgive? (This doesn't mean they deserve it. This is more for you to get relief from having to carry that around as a daily weight.)

3. Have you ever felt defeated? What did you do? Did it work? What, if anything could have been done differently?

4. Do you feel defeated now? What can you do?

5. Journal your thoughts as you re-read Psalm 22:12-22

6. What is your prayer concerning this chapter?

CHAPTER 4

Can't Shake It

And she said, "The Philistines are upon you, Samson!"
So, he awoke from his sleep, and said,
"I will go out as before, at other times, and shake myself free!"
But he did not know that the Lord had departed from him.
JUDGES 16: 20 (NKJV)

It was the summer of 1992. Although I had loved playing my entire football career in my home state of Florida, it was time for a change. Coach Don Shula and I discussed the possibility of a trade to Denver. That trade happened, and I was off to a new city in a new state with a new team. I was officially a Denver Bronco and was looking forward to a fresh start. Obviously, I worked out during the off-season so I could be the best player I could be and contribute my best to my team. The summer of 1992 was no different. It was just a different team and a different workout facility.

With a new team and working out at a new facility, there were new workout partners and trainers. During one late Summer workout at the Broncos facility, I was asked about an exercise that was not particularly my favorite. It was called the Clean and Jerk. Basically, the Clean and Jerk is a composite of three lifting moves combined into one. There's a deadlift, a clean, and an overhead press. The benefit to correctly performing a Clean and Jerk is wide-ranging because it employs so many muscles. It helps with balance and power throughout the body. With all the good it can bring and all the muscles it employs, there's a lot that can go wrong.

I had already hurt my back doing this exercise earlier in my football career and had basically written it off my list of things to do in the gym. But I wanted to improve. I really wanted the explosiveness that could come from doing it. So, I gave it another shot and was making it part of my workout regime. That is, until I hurt myself again. I knew immediately when I did it. The pain rushed through my body. Questions rushed through my mind. *How bad was I hurt? Will it knock me out of pre-season? Will I miss any games?* The thought that didn't cross my mind was… *Will this end my career?*

I had experienced a pulled groin before, and I had recovered. In my mind this was a nuisance injury and that's all. But six weeks later, I realized this was different. This wasn't just a pulled groin I had experienced and worked through before. It wasn't healing and I wasn't pulling through. I guess it was a little like Samson after his hair was cut, and he thought he could just go out and shake himself and everything would be fine. Just as Samson couldn't shake off the weakness he experienced, I couldn't shake this injury. The rehab wasn't working like before. This was different from a pulled groin I had experienced while running track.

There was no way of knowing this injury would end my career as a running back in the NFL. There was no way to know God had plans for me outside of the NFL that would begin on a different timeline than I had expected. I continued to try to work to shake it off and get back to what I felt I did best, running the football.

There was a point where I felt, or at least hoped that I was game ready. But on the first carry, I knew. The explosiveness and ability to cut that I had before wasn't there. It still wasn't right. I thought I had more work to do, and I was willing to do the work.

I made the decision to get a second opinion and reached out to a trusted provider. Dr. Haney had been our team Dr. at Florida State and I trusted him. After meeting with him, he confirmed there was more going on than I thought. It was more than just a pulled groin. I needed to see a specialist. Dr. Haney placed me with one of the most renowned surgeons in the world. Affiliated with Duke University and the New York Giants, this was the person I needed to see.

During consultation, I was advised that I had two choices. One choice was to cut the muscle and just let it heal. The other involved grafts to reattach it. With the first choice, I was told that I would not be able to run a 4.3 in the forty and wouldn't have the same ability to cut. Obviously, speed and ability to cut are important in carrying the football. I said… "Absolutely not!". I wanted to do everything in my power and take advantage of every resource I had to get back on the field without losing previous ability. After all, I was doing the exercise in the first place to try to get better, not slower with less ability to cut. My choice was to have the surgery with the grafts.

While I knew this would keep me out of football for a while, I was committed to do what was necessary through surgery and hard work through rehab to get back on the field and contribute to my team. There was never a second thought. I was still looking forward to getting back on the field with a fresh start in my career.

After surgery, I started rehab and I worked hard to make it back on the field. It wasn't easy, but the light at the end of the tunnel (getting back to playing football at the highest level) was more important than the pain of working through recovery. In the movies, they talk about Lights – Camera – Action... but there were no lights, no cameras covering my recovery, rehab, and workouts. It was just ACTION. It was just me getting up when it hurt and doing the rehab it would take to try to make it back.

Finally, I was at the point to go for it. Although I still had some pain, I thought I could mask it, work through it, and impress a team enough to sign me as a running back to continue my NFL career. Free Agent tryouts were scheduled. I gave it my best, but I couldn't pass the physical. I couldn't get cleared to play. The pain I thought I could mask or play through was evident. I was told I needed to give it more time to heal and that I needed more rehab.

So, I kept working. I kept doing rehab and I gave it more time to heal properly. But the progress I needed wasn't there. Days turned into weeks, and weeks turned into months. Many months passed and it started to wear on me. At a point, I knew inside that this was the end of the road for my comeback to the NFL. I just couldn't shake it. I had done everything I could do. I couldn't work any harder, I couldn't give it more time. My career as a running back in the NFL was over.

God had given me the ability to play football for my high school team, for the Florida State Seminoles, and in the NFL with the Miami Dolphins. But now, my playing days were over. It was a sad day and hard to accept. But there was good news. My life wasn't over, my purpose had not been extinguished. I just wasn't going to be active playing in the NFL. There was an even bigger game that needed my focus... the Game of Life!

While I couldn't cut and change directions on the football field as before, God had given me the ability to cut and change directions in life. He had something different that He wanted me to do. He had more for me to learn. He had different paths for me to take.

It never was about my ability to shake off another tackler or shake off an injury. It is all about the God-given ability to shake off the enemy and to run with patience the race that He has put before us. I still had a race to run. It just wasn't on a track or a football field.

Fortunately, I had an insurance policy with Lloyd's of London and had the financial ability to change directions and start a new career, one that could provide more impact than anything I could ever do on a football field. My heart was, and is, focused on helping other people.

We all have things to shake off. We all have an enemy who is out to steal, kill and destroy everything in his path. We also all have a Heavenly Father who is giving us the ability to shake off the enemy just as Paul shook the serpent off into the fire. Our Heavenly Father has great and amazing plans for you and me. He has given us great ability to achieve what He has planned for us. In retrospect, it was never about football, but God's amazing and perfect plans for our lives and how we can have a current and eternal positive impact on others.

That's why I'm still running!

That's why I have much better goal lines to cross… better touchdowns to score!

God has given me the opportunity to lay up treasures in Heaven where the trophies won't rust, and thieves won't steal. God handed me the ball, the enemy is blocked, and the goal line is ahead. This is something I never want to shake off! This is eternal!

REFLECTION QUESTIONS

1. Is there anything in your life that you want to shake off?

2. If so, is it there because of something you did or didn't do?

3. What lesson(s) can you learn from the experience?

4. What is your prayer concerning this chapter?

CHAPTER 5

Prime Time In The Shadow

*Be kindly affectionate to one another with brotherly love,
in honor giving preference to one another...*
- ROMANS 12:10 NKJV

Brotherly love is a powerful phrase. When there is descension on a team, even the most talented teams can lose. You may recall the verse that says a house divided cannot stand. But when there is brotherly love, when members of the team, in honor, are giving preference to one another, some amazing things can happen. Let me share a story about Prime-Time Deion Sanders...Coach Prime.

In terms of television, the term *Prime Time* refers to the time of day (middle of the evening) when networks target the largest audience. However, when referring to a person, *Prime Time* means Deion Sanders. We were teammates. While I was doing my best to gain yards for our Florida Seminoles, Deion was doing his best to shut the other team's offense down. He was a force on the field when we played and is known by many as the greatest cornerback in NFL history. He has been known as Neon Deion, Prime Time, and today he is known as *Coach Prime*, head football coach for the Colorado Buffaloes of the Pac-12 Conference.

31

After a stellar college career with the Seminoles Deion was the fifth overall pick in the 1989 NFL Draft, selected by the Atlanta Falcons. During his NFL career, he played in eight Pro Bowls and won two Super Bowls, one with the San Francisco 49'ers and one with the Dallas Cowboys. In 2011, he was inducted into the Pro Football Hall of Fame and the College Football Hall of Fame. While in the NFL, Deion Sanders amassed 512 tackles, 53 interceptions (let that sink in), 1,331 interception return yards, 2,199 punt return yards, 3,523 kickoff return yards, and a total of 22 touchdowns. Of course, those are Pro Football Hall of Fame statistics. But football wasn't his only sport.

Deion also played Major League Baseball for nine years, including stints with the New York Yankees, Atlanta Braves, Cincinnati Reds, and the San Francisco Giants where he hit 39 homeruns, 168 Runs Batted In, and 186 stolen bases. He appeared in the 1992 World Series. He is the only athlete to play in a Super Bowl and a World Series. To say he is a sports star is an understatement. Obviously, he had amazing natural talent, he worked at getting better… and he was fast! He ran the 40-yard dash in 4.27 seconds.

So, naturally, any track coach would want him on the track team. I believe if I were the Table Tennis Coach, I would want him on that team. He agreed to be on our track team at Florida State. Deion and I ran the 4 x 100 Meter Relay with Arthur Blake and Dexter Carter. That was a team! Superstars shine on the field of play… super people shine when nobody is watching.

The 4x100 relay begins with the first runners in staggered positions on a track. They are holding a baton which must be passed on to the next person, and the next until the final person, known as the anchor, receives the baton for the final segment of the race. Generally, the fastest person in the group runs anchor. While I was always known as being fast, Deion was faster.

Although I had been the anchor for the team, it only made sense for Deion to run anchor.

Well, it made sense to everyone but Deion. When our coach asked Deion about running anchor for our team, Deion said *Coach, the anchor position belongs to Sammie. He is our anchor. I will be happy to run another position, but not anchor. That belongs to Sammie.*

Think about it, here's Prime Time / Neon Deion passing on running the position that arrives at the finish line for the glory of the win. Obviously, there are more cameras flashing at the finish line than at during the third segment of the race. Yet, Deion turned it down. Not only did that mean he wouldn't be the one from our team crossing the finish line, but it also meant there was additional work and training for him to do. Not running anchor made it harder for him.

You see, the anchor only has to receive the baton and run. The second and third leg team members not only have to receive the baton from the person handing it off, but they also have to train and be skilled at handing it off at the end of their leg. Deion wasn't looking for the position that would be easiest or in more of the spotlight. Prime Time was taking the shadow. You know why? Because that's who he is in his heart. What he taught the first team he coached at Jackson State and what he will teach the Colorado Buffaloes football team is all about team.

It's good to be in the spotlight. Deion earned the title Prime Time. But he did it with a heart for the game, a heart for leaving everything out on the field, and in secret… he gave up the anchor position and worked harder at his role, because he believed it was the right thing to do.

That's what I call Prime Time!

REFLECTION QUESTIONS

1. Do you feel you are giving preference to other people or only thinking about yourself?

2. Is there anything you need to change? Anything you need to do less of, or more of?

3. What is your prayer concerning this chapter?

CHAPTER 6

Family, Friends, the Lord, and Time

"But why should I fast when he is dead?
Can I bring him back again?
I will go to him one day, but he cannot return to me."
2 SAMUEL 12:23 NLT

B ad news can invade our life at any given moment on any given day. Sometimes that bad news can be expected, as in the case of a loved one going through a long-term illness. But sometimes bad news can come like a lightning bolt and deafening clap of thunder out of seemingly nowhere on a clear bluesky day, and that totally catches us off guard. Obviously, it catches us off guard because we don't walk around every day expecting something horrible to happen. Nor should we. But most of us will experience tragedy or some unexpected devastating news at some point in our lives.

Why does it happen? It happens because we live in a fallen world, and that's what happens in a fallen world. In the book of Job, we read...

How frail is humanity?
How short is life, how full of trouble?
JOB 14:1 NLT

Jesus gave us a warning and a promise in the book of John…

I have told you all this so that you may have peace in me.
Hear on earth you will have many trials and sorrows.
But take heart, because I have overcome the world.
JOHN 16:33 NLT

Tragedy can happen to anyone, even Kings.

King David's child had a deadly illness. David fasted and lay on the ground all night praying that the child would live. The elders were very concerned about David and were in hopes the child would live. But on the seventh day, David's child died.

Nobody wanted to tell the King that his child had died. They were concerned that he would do something drastic since he had not listened to their reasoning concerning his child's illness. But he saw them whispering to each other and perceived that his child had died.

He asked them if the child had died, and they told him.

At that point, David got up from the ground, washed and anointed himself, and changed into fresh clothes. Then he did something totally unexpected. He went into the Tabernacle and worshiped. Then he went back to the palace and ate. The people around him couldn't understand why he did what he did. So, they asked, and King David explained. He said he prayed and fasted in hopes that God would allow his child to live. But now, he said there was no need to fast. David stated that, although his child could not come back to him, he knew that one day he could go to his child. David had an eternal perspective. That is very important for us to consider as we all have trials and sorrows to face. If our only focus is on this life, the many trials and sorrows Jesus said we would face could devastate us. But there is eternity to consider.

Sometimes, as was the case with David, trials and sorrows come because of something we did or didn't do. Many times, that's not the case. Sometimes, bad things just happen; and they happen to good people. We live in a fallen world. Life is frail and can be full of trouble. But as we read in John 16:33, we can find peace in Jesus because He has overcome the world. As much as I might want to completely avoid sorrow in this life, I can't. But I can have peace in Jesus that passes understanding, and so can you.

The story I am about to share with you is very personal and is one of the greatest sorrows I have had to face in my life. It was over thirty years ago but seems like yesterday.

I had just completed my rookie season with the Miami Dolphins. I had gained 659 yards and scored 6 touchdowns. We finished the season with eight wins and eight losses, just one game behind the Buffalo Bills, the Division Champion, and only missed getting a wild card spot in the playoffs by one game. We had started the season with a 27-24 loss to the Bills and ended the season with a 27-24 loss at home to the Kansas City Chiefs on Christmas Eve. We were so close. Yet one game out means you are out. Our season was over.

My wife, at the time, was Angela. She was an amazing mother raising our two children, our young daughter, Jenee, and our newborn son Jerrod who was born on November 19, 1989. I wasn't in Miami the day Jerrod was born because we were playing the Cowboys in Dallas that day. We won the game, but I lost the opportunity to be present at my son's birth.

I had no idea what would happen just two months later. The day was Monday, January 22, 1990. After my first season in the NFL, I had decided to drive from Miami back home to Apopka to visit with friends and family for a couple of days. It was going to be a time to rest and reflect on that first exciting and grueling season as a rookie in the NFL. Angela had planned to stay at home with our children. She was going to take Jerrod to the doctor that day for a scheduled 2-month checkup and infant vaccinations. So, on that fateful Monday I drove three and a half hours to my hometown of Apopka. I just didn't know it would be a fateful day.

I arrived in Apopka late in the afternoon and Angela had everything covered at home. She let me know that Jerrod's checkup went well, and that the doctor said everything seemed to be fine with him. With the good news from home in Miami, I was settling into my time of rest and relaxation with friends in my hometown where I grew up. But all wasn't well. I couldn't explain it, but I knew I couldn't stay in Apopka. I had an epiphany that I needed go home to Miami without delay. Sometimes you just don't know why, but you know what you need to do. I knew I needed to drive back and so I did. I knew it was the Holy Spirit prompting me to go home. I just didn't know why. After my second three-and-a-half-hour drive of the day, I arrived back at home in Miami.

The doctor had told Angela that Jerrod would be drowsy from the vaccine. So, she was letting him sleep. His crib was in our bedroom. After checking on Angela and Jenee, I wanted to see Jerrod. I was so proud as a dad, I just wanted to reach in the crib and touch him. When I did, he wheezed. Something wasn't right. We called EMS so they would be on their way.

A few days prior, Angela had watched a TV show detailing how to give CPR to an infant. She immediately started the process. The paramedics arrived and started going through their protocol. Afterwards, they gave us the bad news. Jerrod was gone. We had lost our little boy because of SIDS.

How could that be? We had done everything right as parents. The doctor had just given us a good report that day that everything seemed to be normal with Jerrod. There was no time for me to lay on the ground and fast and pray as King David did for his child. Angela had done everything possible to save him by applying CPR as she had watched demonstrated on a TV show. Jerrod was just gone. It wasn't anyone's fault. He was just gone. He wouldn't grow up to be the fine young man we had hoped he would be. I would never hand him a football, take a run with him, or teach him about life. His life was over.

Angela and I didn't understand. All we knew is that there was nothing we could do to bring him back. But, as King David stated, we knew we could go to him one day. We knew that our baby boy was in Heaven with Jesus. We just didn't understand why. All we understood is how much we were hurting.

In speaking with Angela about what she would want readers of this book to learn from our experience, she said the following…

In this fallen world, we will face traumas, and different trials and tribulations that nobody wants to face. This was an unimaginable shock. Over time, you learn to manage the pain, but it makes an imprint on your life. When you hear bad news, as we did, you want that news you are being told to be a lie, but somehow you know it's true. There is no point of reference. You never get past it, but you get through it. I think about Jerrod being in Heaven. He is with Jesus and forever in His care… and I will see him again.

I want people who experience those shocking tragedies to know that they are not alone. They can go deeper and explore their spiritual life. There is no shortcut through the pain. Lean on family, friends, and the Lord; and know that time with them will provide comfort and hope.

For me, I want you to know that everything Angela said is true. In some cases, answers never come... at least not in this life. I know every question will be answered in Heaven. One answer came for me in 2013 right before Florida State played Northern Illinois in the Orange Bowl. I had been invited back to Miami to speak at the Orange Bowl FCA Breakfast.

I shared the story of Jerrod. After I spoke, there was a long line of people who wanted to speak with me. After a while, I noticed a couple who was waiting to be last in line to speak with me. When it was their time, they shared that they had just recently lost a child to SIDS and wanted to know how I was able to get through it. At that moment, I had no answer. Then, suddenly, the answer came to me, and I shared it with them. It was not only an answer for them, but it was also an answer for me as well. I realized I wasn't the only one to have a son who died. God, Himself, gave His only Son so that we could be saved and live with Him in Heaven for eternity.

Because of His ultimate sacrifice, we can all be saved.

In the Bible, we read about Abraham who was asked to offer his son as a sacrifice. By faith in God, he began the journey to the place of sacrifice. But when asked by his son, Isaac, where the lamb was for the burnt offering, he replied that God would provide for Himself the lamb for the burnt offering. God provided.

You see, Abraham didn't understand, but he went by faith.

I didn't understand the connection, but I had to walk by faith long before I had any sort of answer. I had to accept something I couldn't change. I realized I had to accept what had happened because, as Angela said, we do live in a fallen world. As Jesus said, in this life we will have many trials and troubles. But He has also overcome the world, and because of that I can have peace. You can have peace. I will see Jerrod again! For now, I will share my story and try to help everyone I can. There is something much better on the other side of this life and God gave His one and only Son so that everyone who believes in Him can have peace and can have eternal life. That means you, me, Jerrod, and all of us.

Reflection Questions

1. What is your internal reaction when you receive bad news?

2. When bad news comes, what is your normal reaction concerning God?

3. When bad news comes, what is your normal reaction concerning others?

4. How can you better prepare your heart for possible bad news?

5. How can you better prepare your heart for possible good news?

6. Journal about a time someone has helped you through receiving bad news.

7. Journal about a time you have helped someone through receiving bad news.

8. How can difficult times strengthen your faith?

9. What is your prayer concerning this chapter?

CONTENDER VS. PRETENDER
FCA CHAPELS
OLE MISS FOOTBALL 2022
GAMES 1-12

In this section we will share devotions based on chapel sessions with the Ole Miss football team during the 2022 season. These devotional sections will be divided into game sections… Game 1 through Game 12.

GAME 1 :

Pride

At the beginning of each season every team has the same record, 0 wins and 0 losses. Last year's champion is just that, last year's champion. That's history. The current season is the one that matters most. Anything can happen during a given year. Pre-season rankings are just guesses. While they can produce pride or even doubt within a team, neither should be present. Each can bring a team down. So, Pride seemed like the best place to start with a new season.

> 23 And whatever you do, do it heartily, as to the Lord and not to men, 24 knowing that from the Lord you will receive the reward of the inheritance; for you serve the Lord Christ. 25 But he who does wrong will be repaid for what he has done, and there is no partiality.
> **COLOSSIANS 3:23-25 (NKJV)**

Whatever you do, work heartily, as for the Lord and not for men...
Football may be called entertainment by many, and in many ways, it is... but that's not all it is. The early morning workouts, bumps, bruises, blood, sweat, and tears left on the practice field

don't always seem like entertainment. In fact, it feels more like a four-letter word… W-O-R-K.

That's because that is exactly what it is… it is work. Although it may sound funny to call work a four-letter word, that doesn't mean it's bad. Think about it. L-O-V-E is a four-letter word. So are the words GOAL, CARE, DAWN, EPIC, FUEL, GAIN, GROW, HOPE, and LIFE… you get the point.

Work is simply defined in the Oxford Dictionary as *activity involving mental or physical effort done in order to achieve a purpose or result.* Work is what it takes to win whether it be in football or life.

So, scripture instructs us to work. But it doesn't stop there. It teaches us to work heartily (with all our heart) at whatever we do. But why? Just to win the applause of other people? No way! In whatever we do, we are to work with all our heart as though we are working for the Lord and not for men. Think about it. If we do everything we do focused on other people and what pleases them, what will that get us? If we work and the results are good, we may be rewarded well. Of course, there is nothing wrong with that. But what else can happen? We can start believing the press reports about what others are saying about us… and pride can slip in.

When that happens, our focus is on us. No longer is it even about serving or pleasing other people. We can become totally self-absorbed and only focus on ourselves. That's when bad things can happen. The focus becomes on now, and the next win. But God has a better way. When we realize that we will receive an inheritance from Him as our reward, there is no place for pride.

We begin to understand that the very strength and ability to succeed come from God. God provides the path and opportunity, and we do work. It always works best that way. Just remember, you are ultimately serving the Lord Christ. That's WHO we want to please because that's when we truly win at life and work.

Note: If there is something you want / need to change, consider Craig Groeschel's book The Power To Change: Mastering the Habits That Matter Most.

> ³ Let nothing be done through selfish ambition or conceit,
> but in lowliness of mind let each esteem others better
> than himself. ⁴ Let each of you look out not only for his own
> interests, but also for the interests of others.
> **PHILIPPIANS 2:3-5 (NKJV)**

Pride has been defined as: *a feeling of deep pleasure or satisfaction derived from one's own achievements, the achievements of those with whom one is closely associated, or from qualities or possessions that are widely admired.*

Consider this, with the game on the line, the team is lined up to kick a 35-yard game-winning field goal. Would you want to have an All-American kicker taking paces back from the point where the ball would be kicked? Of course. But how important is the skill level of the kicker if the holder cannot catch, adjust, and place the ball down after the snap? Or what if there is a bad snap? What if the long snapper can't hit the target? Or what if the line misses their blocking assignments and blockers are rushing in like they are running through turnstiles at the county fair? How important is the kicker then?

Why is the team even kicking a 35-yard field goal and not kicking a 55-yarder? Somebody on the offense got them there. Or should I have used the term somebodies. It wasn't just the quarterback, running back, or receivers. It was the entire team with everyone doing their part. We can keep going back in the game.

Why did the offense even have the ball with the opportunity to get close enough to kick a game-winning field goal. At some point the defense had to prevent the other team from advancing. We could go back to the first play of the game. Every play and every player matters.

You see, it's the team that is significant, not just one player. It's that way in football, in work, in church, and in life. We all matter, and we all need each other. So, what we do should be for the team, not selfish ambition or conceit. You may have heard T.E.A.M. – Together Everyone Achieves More.

True champions are Hungry, Humble, and Smart.

Note: For more in depth information, consider Pat Lencioni's book, The Ideal Team Player.

> 18 Pride goes before destruction,
> And a haughty spirit before a fall.
> 19 Better to be of a humble spirit with the lowly,
> Than to divide the spoil with the proud.
> **PROVERBS 16:18-19 (NKJV)**

Pride goes before destruction, and a haughty spirit before a fall. That sounds simple enough.

For whatever reason, many people quote this scripture out of order. I've heard many people say *Pride comes before a fall.* However, it says *Pride comes before destruction...*

Think about this... while you may have heard about the SS Titanic, you may have never heard about a ship named the SS Mesaba. On April 15, 1912, the Captain of the Titanic was warned. The crew of the SS Mesaba sent a radio warning message to Titanic Captain Edward Smith warning him of rogue icebergs drifting around the coast of Newfoundland. The message was received, but never acted on. Over 1,500 people died when the Titanic sank.

Why? Maybe it was because the Titanic was thought to be unsinkable. Maybe it was pride that went before the destruction of the Titanic and the needless loss of lives. Before its first voyage, an engineering journal claimed that the Titanic was "practically unsinkable". Pride grew. Although it is debatable who said it, someone claimed to have heard Captain Edward Smith say, "Even God Himself couldn't sink this ship." Whether he said it, or someone else, the warning by the SS Mesaba was not acted on, and the Titanic was lost. Pride goes before destruction and a haughty spirit before a fall.

It's best to leave pride where it belongs... on the trash heaps of destruction.

Note: Titanic information used in this devotion was taken from https://www.nbcnews.com/id/wbna46916279

Reflection Questions

1. Are there areas in your life where you are dealing with pride?

2. If so, what can / should you do?

3. Journal your thoughts concerning Colossians 3:23-25.

4. Journal your thoughts concerning Philippians 2:3-5.

5. Journal your thoughts concerning Proverbs 16:18-19.

6. What is your prayer concerning this chapter?

GAME 2:

Passionate & Patient / Passive Procrastinator

Therefore, whether you eat or drink, or whatever you do,
do all to the glory of God.
1 Cor. 10:31 (NKJV)

The first two words of the title may sound like an oxymoron. According to grammarly.com, an oxymoron is: *a figure of speech that combines contradictory words with opposing meanings, like "old news," "deafening silence," or "organized chaos."* How can you be both passionate and patient?

First, for followers of Jesus Christ, it's always best to run everything through the filter of 1 Cor. 10:13… doing everything to the glory of God. That takes our personal preferences for timing out of the equation. Many times, a passionate person wants to do something or accomplish something right now. Why wait? But wait… (See what I did there?) There is more to consider. It's not just what we do, but how we do it, the heart behind our action… and when we do it.

Consider Jesus. As we read in scripture, although He was passionate about His mission on earth, he was patient. At a point, although He was urged to go to Judea for his disciples to see the work He was doing, Jesus said: *My time has not yet come.* Timing was and is important to Him. When a group of people told Him Lazarus was sick, He didn't immediately drop everything and go to him. In fact, He told the group that it was better that He was not there when Lazarus died. Everything He did was done with the highest level of passion, but He was never rushed. He was, and is, Passionate and Patient.

However, He was certainly not a Passive Procrastinator. He was passionate but not passive. He was patient and never procrastinated. He was never late in fulfilling His mission.

In life, we can all experience those times when urgency rules the day. Many times, that urgency was brought about by procrastination. I remember reading a sign that said: *Poor planning on your part does not constitute an emergency on my part.* Most, if not all of us, have procrastinated something that should have been done sooner. Most, if not all of us have been driven by the pressure or urgency because of our delaying action. That causes undue pressure that can even cause accidents and / or bring on illness. But that doesn't have to be the case.

Remember the *What Would Jesus Do* bracelets? That is still a great question today. In any endeavor, you can ask yourself a few great questions:

What would a passionate patient person do in this situation?

How can being passionate and patient be helpful in this situation?

What is the danger of letting passion override patience?

What is the danger in letting patience evolve into procrastination?

How can I be passive about this if it's truly important?

The opening verse for the Game 2 Devotion is:

> Therefore, whether you eat or drink, or whatever you do,
> do all to the glory of God.
> **1 COR. 10:31 (NKJV)**

There is nothing passive about doing something for the glory of God.

Yet, God is patient.

Imagine you are standing with Jesus when someone comes from Bethany, the village where Jesus' friend Lazarus lived with his sisters Mary and Martha. Maybe you were also with Jesus when Mary had poured very expensive perfume on the feet of Jesus and wiped it with her hair. You know about the connection among these friends. Suddenly, you realize this person is not coming to greet Jesus or to share with him good news from his friends. So, you move in a little closer and overhear Jesus being told that Martha and Mary had sent him to tell Jesus that Lazarus was very sick. Your first thought might be... what will Jesus do? Afterall, He is the Son of God and can do anything.

You may have heard how He has healed the sick. He has made the lame to walk, the deaf to hear, and the blind to see. Nothing is impossible for him. He could speak the word and Lazarus would be healed. He could snap His finger and immediately be standing in Bethany where His friend Lazarus was suffering. But that's not what He did. He did say the sickness of Lazarus would not end in death, but for God's glory so God's Son may be glorified through it. Yet, He still didn't rush to Lazarus' side to heal him. In fact, He stayed where he was for two more days.

After two days, He said: *let's go back to Judea. John 11:7 (NLT).*

Finally!

Bethany is in Judea. Lazarus is sick in Bethany. While he was passionate about his friend Lazarus, Jesus was patient and waited two days before starting out for Judea. After all, Jesus said the sickness Lazarus had would not end in death, but in the glory of God. He intentionally waited.

But by the time He arrived in Bethany, He was told, although He already knew, that Lazarus had been in the tomb for four days! Martha heard that Jesus was coming, so she went out to meet Him. Mary stayed at home. Think about that, for a minute. Why did Mary stay home? Was it because she was upset that Jesus had not come earlier? Possibly. He had not been there to heal Lazarus, and Lazarus had died. We do know why Martha went to greet Jesus. Scripture is clear on the first recorded words she said to Him.

After calling Him Lord, she said if He had been there, Lazarus would not have died. Mary stayed home, but Martha marched right up to Jesus and told Him what she thought. They believed that His delay (patience) had cost Lazarus his life. Oh, and what about that statement that this sickness would not end in death, but for the glory of God. The fact was that by now (after four days in the tomb), Lazarus stinketh! Ok, so we grabbed a little King James English for that one. Other versions say that by now, there is a bad order. Either way, you get the picture. The fact remains. Jesus heard Lazarus was sick, but he waited two days before starting to make His way to Lazarus. Had He been too patient? Had He miscalculated and now it was too late? Nope! A thousand times no!

Remember, He said it wouldn't end in death. He never said Lazarus would not die. Let that sink in for a moment. He knew what He was doing, and He was patient doing it. He then told

Martha that Lazarus would live again. Martha believed Him. He knew exactly what He was doing. He had been patient for a reason.

Martha went back and called Mary aside to let her know Jesus was there and was asking for her. At that point, Mary immediately went to see Jesus. People in the house comforting Mary at that time saw her quickly leave. They followed her as they thought she was going to the tomb to mourn. But when Mary reached the place where Jesus was, she fell at His feet. Then she said the same thing Martha had said earlier. She said that if Jesus had been there, her brother Lazarus would not have died. Jesus asked where they had laid Lazarus. They invited Jesus to come and see where Lazarus had been laid. At that point, the shortest verse in the Bible was recorded… the two words: "Jesus wept."

Some of the people present mentioned the love Jesus must have had for His friend, Lazarus. Others questioned why Jesus, who had healed others, had not prevented Lazarus from dying. Jesus told them to move the stone away from the entrance. That's when Martha mentioned the possibility (actually, a probability) of an odor from a dead man being in a tomb for four days. Jesus prayed a short prayer and then, in a loud voice, called for Lazarus to come out.

Lazarus walked out of the tomb. Jesus instructed the people to take the grave clothes off him and let him go. Martha, Mary, and others present that day learned a valuable lesson. He is an on-time God! He is passionate and patient. He is not a passive procrastinator. As followers of Christ, we should all be passionate and patient, and never be a passive procrastinator.

REFLECTION QUESTIONS

1. Journal your thoughts concerning 1 Corinthians 10:31.

2. Are there areas in your life where you should have more passion?

3. Are there areas in your life where you should be more patient?

4. Journal your thoughts about how Jesus had passion and patience and how that could be helpful in your life?

5. What is your prayer concerning this chapter?

GAME 3:

Challenges

Then David said to the Philistine, "You have come to me with a sword and a spear and with a javelin, but I come to you in the name of the Lord of hosts, the God of the armies of Israel, whom you have defied. This day the Lord will deliver you into my hand, and I will strike you down..."
1 Samuel 17: 45-46 ESV

And she said, "The Philistines are upon you, Samson!" And he awoke from his sleep and said, "I will go out as at other times and shake myself free." But he did not know that the Lord had left him. And the Philistines seized him and gouged out his eyes and brought him down to Gaza and bound him with bronze shackles. And he ground at the mill in the prison.
Judges 16:20-21 ESV

God's Word is a book of stories. They are stories of people who had challenges. We all do. Life is full of challenges. It's been said that you are either coming out of a challenge, in the middle of a challenge, or about to go into a challenge every day you live on earth. Life is a challenge. A football game is a challenge. Everything is a challenge.

There are four questions to consider when thinking about challenges:

What is the challenge?

Why am I in this challenge?

How can I win the challenge?

Win or lose, what can I learn from the challenge?

You can use these four questions for any challenge you may face.

The verses above depict two very different challenges. One is of David and Goliath the giant, and the other is of Samson when he lost his strength. Let's consider the four questions for each challenge.

David and Goliath

What was David's challenge?

As a young boy, David's dad sent him to carry some grain and cheese to where his brothers were camped with King Saul. His dad also asked him to check on his brothers to see how they are doing and report back to him. When David arrived, he saw that there was a giant coming out every day to challenge the army and no one would stand up to him. David took that on as a challenge. He was young, small, and inexperienced with the King and his brothers' instruments of war. Yet he was ready to accept the challenge and face the giant.

Goliath was really coming out against God. David had seen what God could do as He had already helped David kill a bear and a lion while he was shepherding sheep. David was standing up against the giant who was defying the army of God. David voluntarily stepped into the challenge.

Why was David in this challenge?

David stepped into this challenge when he saw what the giant was doing and how the army of Israel had responded. You might say, David asked for the challenge… because he did.

How could David win the challenge?

David told King Saul that God has rescued him from the paw of a bear and the paw of a lion, and that God would rescue him from the giant. He would not wear the armor that he was not familiar with but would take his sling. He picked up 5 smooth stones and went toward the challenge.

What can we learn from David's challenge?

Once again, David saw that God was faithful. David did what he could with what he had, and God helped. When we walk in faith in God and use what God has given us to use, there is no challenge, no giant too big for us to face because God is faithful.

SAMSON'S CHALLENGE

What was Samson's challenge?

Samson was captured by his enemies and blinded. He was held prisoner grinding grain in a Gaza prison. He had quickly gone from being the strongest man in the world, conquering enemies with ease, to being a prisoner without the ability to see.

Why was Samson in this challenge?

In short, Samson landed himself in this challenge. While many things Samson did led to his being blinded and held captive, the culmination of it all came as he was with his Philistine girlfriend named Delilah. She was paid the equivalent of three years wages to discover the secret of Samson's strength so his enemies could overcome him and take him captive.

Through a series of events, he should have known what she was doing. But Samson had already been blinded in his mind well before his eyes were plucked out. Isn't that the way with us sometimes? It's easy to go back in time and see where we should have known better than to do the wrong things we did.

How could Samson win this challenge?

There is an easy answer. It would have been better for Samson not to be in this challenge. He brought it on himself by going against the wisdom and instruction he had been given. You might say, in this case, Samson was playing too close to the fire and got burned. Many times we all want to see how close to the edge we can get without crossing a line. When that happens, the lines get blurred, and we cross the line before we know it.

However, once he was in the challenge caused by his own volition, he did the only thing he could do… call out to God for help. If you ever find yourself in that situation, repent (turn away from what is wrong), and just ask for help. Scripture teaches us that God is a present help in time of need.

What can we learn from Samson's challenge?

There is good news. God can and will forgive us for the sins we have committed. He also can and will use us for good despite our wrongdoing. First comes repentance, which begins with admitting we were wrong, and turning away from it. We have all done wrong. Scripture clearly states that we have all sinned and fall short of the glory of God. While that may be hard to hear (or read) we all know it is true. The good news, that we call the Gospel, is that there is hope in Jesus Christ. The next verse tells us that we can be *justified freely by His grace through the redemption that is in Christ Jesus.* (Romans 3:24 NKJV)

We all have challenges from time to time, some are self-imposed (brought about because of our own action or inaction) and some just happen because of normal everyday life. So, the question is not whether we will have challenges, but what we do with them when they come. Challenges can make us stronger or can influence us to give up. A challenge is just something that tests your current abilities. Losing a challenge tells you something about your ability. Giving up on a challenge tells you something about your real desire and what is going on inside your mind and your heart. Don't give up, and don't beat yourself up over past failures. Get up, pick up, and face the next challenge with courage and faith.

David and Samson are just two individual people like you and me. Of course, David was a King and Samson slayed a lion with his bare hands and defeated an entire army with only the jawbone of a donkey as a weapon. Yet, they were only human. They had their faults and they each made great mistakes along the way. They both paid heavy prices for their mistakes. But in the end, they won. Samson defeated 3,000 Philistines after he had been captured and blinded. David was known as a man after God's heart as well as being one of the greatest kings in the history of Israel. Before he died, he gave over 112 tons of gold, 262 tons of refined silver, and other building materials for his son Solomon to use in building the temple. (I Chron 29:4 NLT)

The end of your story hasn't been written yet. Like all of us, you have already overcome challenges, and there are more to come. We will all have challenges. What will you do with your own personal challenges, and how can you turn those challenges into victories that will ultimately benefit yourself as well as others?

REFLECTION QUESTIONS

1. What can you learn from how David and Samson handled challenges?

2. What challenges have you overcome in your life? How did you overcome those challenges?

3. What challenges are you still facing?

4. Consider a current challenge you are facing and ask yourself the four questions from the chapter. Journal your responses.

5. What is your prayer concerning this chapter?

GAME 4:

Faith

But without faith it is impossible to please Him,
for he who comes to God must believe that He is,
and that He is a rewarder of those who diligently seek Him.

HEBREWS 11:6 NKJV

So Jesus said to them, "Because of your [a]unbelief; for
assuredly, I say to you, if you have faith as a mustard seed,
you will say to this mountain, 'Move from here to there,' and it
will move; and nothing will be impossible for you.

MATTHEW 17:20 NKJV

What is faith? Why is it important?

Although it might sound simple, these are two of the most important questions to answer. Following up on that is: What do you believe? In other words, what do you believe in?

Is there anyone in whom you have complete trust and confidence?

Some people may say they don't have trust or confidence in anything or anybody. But they do. Consider this, when a person walks into a dark room and flips the light switch to the "ON" position, are they surprised when the lights come on or surprised if they don't? Obviously, they are surprised when they don't. Immediately, they try to discern why the lights didn't come on. Is the electricity on? Did I pay the light bill this month? Could there be a light bulb that is burned out? Is the switch not working? There must be a reason the light didn't come on.

However, absolutely nothing concerning the light prompts thoughts about why it came on when it did. There is no contemplation of how electricity is generated, how it comes into the house, how the switch works, or what makes a light bulb burn. There is no concern about whether the electric bill was paid for the previous month. They just flip the light switch on and go their merry way. You know why? It's because they have faith. They have faith that the electricity is on, the light switch works, and the bulb is not burned out. They just believe.

Have you ever asked your Dr. where he or she went to medical school? Have you ever asked to see their framed diploma? Or have you ever asked to see their transcript to see what grades they made before you trust their opinion or trust them to perform a procedure on your body? No. At least I have never heard of anyone who has done that before. One time a surgeon asked if anyone has ever considered what they call a person who finishes dead last in their medical school class? (Did you catch the pun there? It was intended.) After a moment, the surgeon responded: Doctor! That's right, someone finished with the lowest grades in their medical school class, and that person is called Doctor. Is that your doctor? My guess is that you have never asked.

The truth, and the good news, is that you don't have to ask. But there is a reason. You don't feel the need to ask because you believe (or have faith in the fact that) medical schools don't pass people who can't (or shouldn't) be doctors. Medical Boards won't allow people to be certified who haven't passed certain criteria. There again, people have faith that their doctor can help with medical issues. They believe in the doctor's training and ability to help. That is faith.

If we can believe in a light switch, a light bulb, and the electric company... if we can believe in a doctor or other medical care provider, we can certainly believe in God. Scripture says that, without faith, it is impossible to please Him. That's what he wants from us. He wants us to believe Him. He wants us to believe what He says is true, and for us to obey His word because we believe in Him. He wants us to believe that He is God, and that He is a rewarder of those who diligently seek Him.

He is God. He is the creator of everything. He is all powerful and nothing is impossible for Him. He created the ability for us to have lights in our houses. He gave doctors and medical schools the knowledge needed to help us with medical issues. Yet, no one has all power and all knowledge as God. Only God has that! Many times, doctors have told families they have done all they can do. They have tried everything in their knowledge that they can do to help. Many times, they have been surprised by a supernatural work that has been done because someone had faith and prayed and had asked God for help, and He did what the doctors couldn't do.

How much faith is required?

You may have heard of people throughout history who have been said to have great faith. That's because their faith has grown. Over time, they have become to believe more and more in what God is doing, even when it doesn't seem to work out the way they want it to work out. They have learned to believe and trust in God beyond their own ability to understand.

But how much faith is needed?

Do you need a tablespoon full of faith, or a cup full, or a bowl full? How big is your faith?

In scripture (Matthew 17:20) we find a very interesting passage that speaks of having faith as a mustard seed. It says that if we have faith as a mustard seed, we can speak to and move a mountain. It says if you have faith as a mustard seed, nothing will be impossible for you.

Obviously, God wants us to have faith in Him. As we've read, we can't please Him without faith. But our faith should not be stagnant. He wants it to grow. Consider what is said about a mustard seed and that we should have faith as a mustard seed. Mustard seeds are tiny. They are only about 1-2 millimeters in size. That means that they are generally less than one-tenth of an inch in size. An inch is equal to 24.5 millimeters. In comparison, an apple seed is 8 millimeters in size. Mustard seeds are small... very small. But they grow.

When mustard seeds grow, they grow big enough for birds to make nests in the branches. Think about it. Birds eat seeds and they are gone. Yet, if a mustard seed is planted in a field, and has enough water and sun, it will grow big enough for birds to build their nests in its branches.

You may have a little faith right now, but consider what you really have planted inside you. You have faith that, although it may be small now, it can grow. Just imagine the possibilities! In fact, imagine nothing being impossible. Because, with God, all things are possible.

God's word says: "So then faith comes by hearing, and hearing by the word of God." (Romans 10:17 NKJV) What does that mean? In the example of the mustard seed, it means that a planted seed needs something to grow, and concerning faith, we need the word of God for our faith to grow. We must hear the word of God and we must obey it. When we do, our faith grows.

Reflection Questions

1. Why do you believe it is impossible to please God without faith?

2. What do you believe about Matthew 17:20?

3. Journal your thoughts concerning Romans 10:17.

4. What is your prayer concerning this chapter?

GAME 5:

Significance

¹⁸ And Jesus, walking by the Sea of Galilee, saw two brothers,
Simon called Peter, and Andrew his brother, casting a net into
the sea for they were fishermen.
¹⁹ Then He said to them, "Follow Me, and I will make
you fishers of men."
²⁰ They immediately left their nets and followed Him.
MATTHEW 4:18-22 NKJV

Accoring to Merriam-Webster online, one definition of significance is *the quality of being important.* It also *implies a quality or character that should mark a thing as important but that is not self-evident and may or may not be recognized.*

Think about that for a minute. What does important really mean? Why is something considered important? Now, consider Jesus as he was walking by the Sea of Galilee and seeing two brothers, Simon called Peter, and Andrew fishing. They were just two guys casting a net into the sea. Just doing what fishermen do.

Why did He even stop to talk with them? Why did they stop fishing to talk with him? Afterall, they were busy fishing. As fishermen, that was their job. No fish meant no money; and yet they stopped to speak with Him. What came next is strange, yet beautiful.

Consider for a moment what could have happened between verses 19 and 20. In verse 18, Jesus sees Simon and Andrew fishing. In verse 19, without introduction or small talk, He asks them to follow Him and tells them He will make them fishers of men. What would you have said? I believe I would have had some questions if someone interrupts my work and asks me to follow them.

Many people could and probably would have questions including the following:

- Why me? Why my brother?
- You want both of us?
- What should we do with our nets?
- How will we explain this to people back home?
- Why follow you?
- Where are you going?
- How long will we be gone?
- Who will pay my bills while I'm gone?
- Will you be paying us for this fishing of men?
- What else is in it for me?
- What do you mean by making us "fishers of men"?
- What do we do when we catch them? (Joking, of course.)
- How long do we have to think about it?
- Will anyone else be doing this?
- How many have already turned you down?
- Can we tell you later?

Ok, you get the point.

Something strange happened between verses 19 and 20. The strange thing that happened between those two verses is... nothing. That's right, nothing happened between the two verses. They didn't even ask one question. However, the one thing that is easy to miss is that He didn't ASK them to go with Him. It wasn't something like: *Hey guys, how about following me and I will make you fishers of men?* It wasn't a question. Maybe that was implied, but it wasn't asked in a question. Verse 19 states: Then He said to them, *Follow Me and I will make you fishers of men.*

But why? Why did nothing happen between verses 19 and 20? Why did they just drop their nets and follow Jesus when he asked? The answer is there is more to this story than we read in that one passage.

The answer may be found in John 1:40-43 NKJV.

40 One of the two who heard John speak, and followed Him, was Andrew, Simon Peter's brother.

41 He first found his own brother Simon, and said to him, "We have found the Messiah" (which is translated, the Christ).

42 And he brought him to Jesus. Now when Jesus looked at him, He said, "You are Simon the son of Jonah. You shall be called Cephas" (which is translated 'A Stone'.)

43 The following day Jesus wanted to go to Galilee...

That explains it! Obviously, the encounter on the day they were fishing wasn't their first encounter with Jesus. First Andrew, then his brother Simon, had met Jesus already and realized they have found the Messiah. It wasn't just anyone making the statement to them to come follow Him and He would make them fishers of men. It was THE Messiah!

He was calling them. By leaving their nets and following Him, they were on a mission from God. That one detail changes everything! What He was calling them to do was something significant. He was calling them into a life of significance. Now, what they were about to do had the quality of being important. By only reading part of the story, it was not self-evident or easily recognizable that they were about to be world changers. But when you know the rest of the story, it all fits together like a beautiful jigsaw puzzle.

Isn't that how things happen in life? We don't always know the whole story. We may believe we are living a life of insignificance, a life of little or no importance. The enemy will lie to us saying that we are living a meaningless life. But that's just not true. We all have purpose. You have purpose, your life has meaning. In fact, you may have already done something so significant that it has a positive impact on hundreds of thousands, or maybe millions of lives and you just don't know it… yet.

Consider this.

> ³⁴ *Then the King will say to those on His right hand, 'Come, you blessed of My Father, inherit the kingdom prepared for you from the foundation of the world:* ³⁵ *for I was hungry and you gave Me food; I was thirsty and you gave Me drink; I was a stranger and you took Me in;* ³⁶ *I was naked and you clothed Me; I was sick and you visited Me; I was in prison and you came to Me.' – Matthew 25:34-36 (NKJV)*

With a glimpse of the final judgment, when everything gets sorted out, we see the King separating people to the right and left. To those on his right hand, he calls them blessed and allows them to inherit the kingdom prepared from the foundation of the world. Then he adds an interesting statement. He says, I was hungry, and you gave Me food, I was thirsty, and you gave Me drink, I was a stranger, and you took Me in, naked and you clothed Me, sick and you visited Me, and in prison and you came to Me. Obviously, nobody had seen the King in those situations.

The righteous responded by asking when they had seen the King in those situations and when they had done those things unto Him. He said, as you did it unto the least of these, you did it unto Me. What a statement! What they thought had been an insignificant gift of food or drink, an uneventful offer to take someone in, a kind offer of a shirt or coat, a simple visit to the sick or someone in prison had been recorded as something significant in Heaven. That's right! They had been doing something significant even when they didn't realize it.

The same goes for you. While you may have forgotten what you thought was an insignificant act of kindness, something you have already done may be recorded in Heaven, just waiting for the King to remind you of it one day. Maybe something you will do tomorrow will be remembered forever.

No act of kindness is too small for God to see! Now, go do something significant!

Reflection Questions

1. What are the 5 most significant / important things in your life? (This could also include people.)

2. Why do you believe Simon and Andrew immediately left their nets and followed Jesus?

3. What questions would you have had if you had been there with Simon and Andrew and heard Jesus call out to you? Would you have followed? Why? Why not?

4. What do you want to hear from God on Judgment Day?

5. What is your prayer concerning this chapter?

6. Do you believe you could be living your life with more significance? If so, see the Irrefutable Success University page and QR code on page 123 in this book for more information and a free month of Irrefutable Success University.

GAME 6:

Resilience

A marathon is a 26-mile and 385-yard (42.195 km) race based on a Greek legend. While many run the race, it can be completed with a run / walk strategy. Either way, it is a very long distance that requires resilience to finish. The legend is based on a run that was completed by someone named Pheidippides, a messenger for the Greek army, after The Battle of Marathon in 490 BC.

Pheidippides ran from the town of Marathon back to Athens to report the Athenian army's victory over the invading Persian army. While there are many versions of the story, the general agreement is that he ran the entire distance then collapsed and died on the spot after he arrived. It has been said that he ditched his weapons and even his clothes to get to Athens in less time. You might say that he made the decision to *lay aside every weight… and run with endurance the race that was set before him* (see Hebrews 12:1).

But why the rush to Athens to report a victory in battle? One version states that he had noticed a Persian ship changing course to make its way to Athens. In this case, he may have perceived that the ship was going to report that the Persians had won The Battle of Marathon so that the people in Athens would lose heart and possibly submit to the Persians. Maybe that was why he felt a sense of urgency to run the distance. Whatever the reason, he ran. He ran on purpose, and he made it to Athens.

Other than the news of victory that he was carrying, he left everything else behind and reached forward to what was ahead. His goal was to reach Athens. Paul's was to *press toward the goal for the prize of the upward call of God.* (Philippians 3:14) That should be ours. But just as with Pheidippides or any marathon runner, running our race will take resilience (the strength and ability to recover) because we will face obstacles.

While we don't specifically know the obstacles Pheidippides faced, we know that every race has obstacles. Some races, like Spartan races, have obstacles built into the race, while other races have natural obstacles. There is always weather, terrain, and our own natural tendencies to give up that must be negotiated along the course of any race… including the course of our own lives.

According to the Oxford dictionary, resilience is the capacity to withstand, or recover quickly from difficulties. Sometimes the inside battles are the hardest. Here's a quote from the book *Every Day is Game Day*… If you lose the battle on the inside, you are in grave danger of losing the war that manifests itself on the outside. If you start believing things are too hard, or you are too tired, or running the race is not important, you are setting yourself up to quit. Quitting is not finishing. Quitting is accepting loss. Quitting is giving up on victory.

Jim Rohn once said: *Don't wish things were easier, wish you were better.*

In 1 Corinthians 9:24 (NKJV), we read:

Do you not know that those who run in a race all run, but one receives the prize? Run in such a way that you may obtain it.

No prize is obtained by quitting. God's word instructs us to run in such a way to obtain. In this race, we must have resilience to keep running.

It's easier to give up than to persevere.

In his poem, *Don't Quit*, Edgar A. Guest said: *Success is failure turned inside out.*

There will always be one more mile to run, one more mountain to climb, one more valley to go through, one more challenge to overcome. The end is the end. Until then, we must have the resilience to continue.

One of the greatest stories of resilience we find in scripture is that of Job.

In the book of Job, in the first verse of the first chapter, we find:

There was a man in the land of Uz, whose name was Job…

Scripture teaches us that Job was a man who God said was blameless and upright. He was a man who feared God and shunned evil. Yet, it was allowed for him to go through a very rough patch in life. In fact, it got so bad for Job that he got up, tore his robe, shaved his head, and fell to the ground and worshiped. It was either that, or completely give up.

In fact, at one point, Job's wife suggested that he curse God and die and his group of friends brought accusations against him that he had sinned and needed to repent.

But Job had resilience. He had the power to overcome the obstacles he was facing.

He listened to what his wife had suggested, then responded with:

> You speak as one of the foolish women speaks. Shall we indeed accept good from God, and shall we not accept adversity? Job 2:10 (NJKV)

He listened to his friends, inquired about their motives, and defended his faithfulness.

He was resilient.

In the end, God gave Job twice as much as he had in the beginning.

Job's resilience and faithfulness was rewarded. Yours will be too!

It's easy to get tired and easy to give up, but as we are instructed in Galatians 6:9, we are not to *grow weary in well doing*, and that *in due season, we will reap if we don't lose heart.* (NKJV)

While that may be impossible in the natural, we know that what is impossible for man is possible for God. There is nothing impossible for Him. With that, He gives us the path to overcome.

It's simple, we take it to Jesus.

²⁸ Come to Me, all you who labor and are heavy laden, and I will give you rest. ²⁹ Take My yoke upon you and learn from Me, for I am gentle and lowly in heart, and you will find rest for your souls. ³⁰ For My yoke is easy and My burden is light." – Matthew 11:28-30 (NKJV)

Reflection Questions

1. Journal your thoughts concerning Philippians 3:13-14.

2. What things do you need to forget, or leave behind?

3. What are you reaching forward to?

4. What are you doing to keep from losing heart along the way?

5. What is your prayer concerning this chapter?

GAME 7:

All In

DAVID'S MIGHTY MEN OF VALOR

¹⁵ And David said with longing, "Oh, that someone would give me a drink of the water from the well of Bethlehem, which is by the gate!"
¹⁶ So the three mighty men broke through the camp of the Philistines, drew water from the well of Bethlehem that was by the gate, and took it and brought it to David. Nevertheless, he would not drink it, but poured it out to the Lord.
2 SAMUEL 23: 15–16 NKJV

²⁰ Benaiah was the son of Jehoiada, the son of a valiant man from Kabzeel, who had done many deeds. He had killed two lion-like heroes of Moab. He also had gone down and killed a lion in the midst of a pit on a snowy day.
2 SAMUEL 23:20 NKJV

⁸ Now Amalek came and fought with Israel in Rephidim.
⁹ And Moses said to Joshua, "Choose us some men and go out,

fight with Amalek. Tomorrow I will stand on the top of the hill with the rod of God in my hand."

¹⁰ So Joshua did as Moses said to him, and fought with Amalek. And Moses, Aaron, and Hur went up to the top of the hill.

¹¹ And so it was, when Moses held up his hand, that Israel prevailed; and when he let down his hand, Amalek prevailed.

¹² But Moses' hands became heavy; so they took a stone and put it under him, and he sat on it. And Aaron and Hur supported his hands, one on one side, and the other on the other side; and his hands were steady until the going down of the sun.

¹³ So Joshua defeated Amalek and his people with the edge of the sword.

Exodus 17:8-13

What does it mean to be All In? A great resource for this topic is the book, *All In: You Are One Decision Away From A Totally Different Life* by Mark Batterson. Have you ever considered the fact that, if something is God's will, God is always All In? He never halfway does anything. The concept of being All In is found throughout scripture. From creation to judgment, and throughout eternity, if it's His will, God is All In.

We should be all in too? In fact, that's how we are instructed by God to live our lives. Consider the following words form Colossians 3:23-24 (NKJV).

²³ *And whatever you do, do it heartily, as to the Lord and not to men,*

²⁴ *knowing that from the Lord you will receive the reward of the inheritance; for you serve the Lord Christ.*

As we mentioned in Game 1, that verse says in whatever we do, we should do it heartily (willingly) as though we are doing it for God and not for men or other people. Imagine that, in whatever you do, you should do it as though you are on a mission for God… because you are. He has given us a mission and whatever we do is important. That means whether we eat or drink, or whatever you do, you should do it for the glory of God. Yep, there is a verse for that too! It's one of the verses we mentioned in Game 2.

> [31] So whether you eat or drink, or whatever you do,
> do it all for the glory of God.
> **1 COR. 10:31 (NKJV)**

Do you think God cares about us being All In? He sure does!

King David had a group of men who were called Men of Valor. One day he was thirsty. Have you ever been hungry or thirsty and wanted something specific? That's the way it was with David that day. He was longing for a drink of water from the well of Bethlehem. There was just something about the water from that specific well that he desired. But it wasn't just any well in Bethlehem, it was the well by the gate.

There was a problem. Between where they were and the well by that gate, there was an enemy camp. The Philistines were there, and they had no plans to share the water from that well with David or his men. But King David's men cared so much about him that they were All In to get some of that water to him. The enemy was just in the way.

So, they broke through the camp of the Philistines and drew some water from the one well King David described and brought it back to him. All that for just one drink of water? Yes, but there is more to consider. It was all that because they were All In for their

King. All he had to do was to mention that he wanted a drink of water from that well and they were on their way.

Now, you might ask... Why didn't he drink it? Did he not want it? Yes, he wanted it. But, read the verse again. It says that he poured it out to the Lord. As much as he wanted that water, and as much as he appreciated the risk his men took to get it, David was All In for God. He poured it out as an offering. The next time you are about to give in the offering, think about being All In.

A few verses later in that passage, we read about Benaiah who was the son of Jehoiada, the son of "a valiant man" from Kabzeel. He was another mighty man who was All In. On one snowy day, he chased a lion into a pit and killed it. Think about that for a minute. If you were camping and a lion came around, you might be really quiet, try to hide, and hope he doesn't attack. Benaiah was just the opposite. He saw a lion and attacked it. We don't know the details of why he was chasing the lion. Maybe it had already attacked his family or neighbors. The reason is not important at this point. We just know that, for whatever reason, he was All In. The lion was the one running away while he chased it into a pit and killed it. That's All In!

There are many ways to be All In. As we have considered, David's men were All In when they broke through enemy lines to get water for him, Benaiah was all in chasing the lion into the pit. In each case, the ones being All In were active in doing something that took them away from where they were. In Exodus 17, we find a group of people who were All In, but in different ways. Moses asked Joshua to choose men to fight Amalek the next day. Joshua did that. The next day, they were All In the battle. Moses stood on top of a hill holding the rod of God in his hand. Although he wasn't in the physical battle below, he was All In.

As long as Moses would hold his hand up, Israel would win. When he dropped his hand, they would begin to lose. That sounds simple enough. For whatever reason, God would allow the battle to depend on whether Moses held his hand in the air. But his hands became heavy, and he expended all the energy he could to just keep his hands raised. He was All In and doing all he could do, but he was physically unable to continue. Fortunately, he wasn't alone. Aaron and Hur were with him. They realized what was going on and came to the rescue.

Aaron and Hur placed a stone where Moses could sit. Then they each held one of his hands up until evening. They were All In, doing what they were doing as unto God and for the glory of God and the victory of Israel. You might think they weren't on the battlefield, but they were. Had they not done what they were doing, Israel could have lost that battle. No matter where you are, or what you are doing, it can be vastly important. Don't minimize your ability to do something… and whatever you do, do it as unto God and not men, and do it all for the glory of God. Be All In!

Reflection Questions

1. Journal your thoughts concerning 2 Samuel 23:15-16.

2. Consider David (2 Samuel 23:15-16). Have you ever longed for something like the water from the well by the gate in Bethlehem, and someone gave to you what you longed for at that time? If so, what was it? How did it make you feel? Specifically, how did it make you feel toward that person?

3. Have you ever provided for another person as David's mighty men of valor did for David? How did that make you feel?

4. Have you ever supported someone else as Aaron and Hur supported Moses? How did that make you feel? How was that person helped?

5. Have you ever been supported by another person as Aaron and Hur supported Moses? How did that make you feel?

6. Like Benaiah (2 Samuel 23:20) what lion in your life would you chase into a pit on a snowy day?

7. What is your prayer concerning this chapter?

GAME 8:

A Certain Peace

²⁷ Peace I leave with you, My peace I give to you; not as the
world gives do I give to you. Let not your heart be troubled,
neither let it be afraid.
JOHN 14:27 (NKJV)

You may have seen a church sign that reads: *No Jesus, No
Peace – Know Jesus, Know Peace*. I love the play on words.
It's called a homophone. That means there are two or more
words with different meanings or spellings that sound the same.
The statement is true. In John 14, Jesus told us that he was leaving
us with peace and the peace He is leaving us with is His peace.
He explained that the peace He is leaving with us is not the same
as the peace the world gives. The world's peace is temporary and
superficial. Then He instructs us to not let our heart be troubled
or afraid.

In life, there are many things that go bump in the night. But,
it's not just in the night. Life can be scary. There are many things
that trouble people's hearts. Some are real and some are just based
on thoughts that pass through our minds. There is fear of the

known and fear of the unknown. Either way, fear takes the place of peace.

The question has been asked, *Where does darkness go when the lights are turned on?* The simple answer is that it races to the outside edge of the light. That's true. Darkness cannot override light. When God said let there be light, there was light, and darkness had to go to the outside edge of the light. If you've ever been on a plane flying north or south at the end or beginning of the day, you may have seen darkness (or night) on one side and light (or day) on the other. Obviously, there is not a distinct line between night and day, it's gradual. But the truth is that when the sun shines in, darkness must depart.

Darkness doesn't have a source. Darkness is the absence of light. Light is not the absence of darkness because light has a source. When that source is present, darkness has to flee away from that source.

It's the same with the difference of a heart full of peace and a heart that is troubled and afraid. Jesus is our source of peace. If we have His peace, the darkness of a troubled or fearful heart must leave. When He speaks peace, you may still be on a boat in the water, but the fear of the storm is over.

Consider this passage in Mark 4 (NKJV)

35 On the same day, when evening had come, He said to them, "Let us cross over to the other side." 36 Now when they had left the multitude, they took Him along in the boat as He was. And other little boats were also with Him. 37 And a great windstorm arose, and the waves beat into the boat, so that it was already filling. 38 But He was in the stern, asleep on a pillow. And they awoke Him and said to Him, "Teacher, do You not care that we are perishing?"

There are some facts to consider with that passage. A great windstorm arose. It's one thing to be on shore with a great windstorm. It's quite another to be in a boat far from shore when the winds are raging, and the waves begin to beat into the boat. A rocky boat isn't fun… a rocky boat with waves beating into the boat and filling it up with water is a crisis! That might be a good cue to be afraid.

Where was Jesus?

Well, He wasn't afraid. In fact, he was sleeping on a pillow in the stern of the ship.

Didn't He care that they were perishing? Great question! That's what they asked after they woke him. *Teacher, do You not care that we are perishing?*

There are many things He could have said to them. The conversation could have gone as follows:

Jesus: *Hey guys, what did I say before we got into the boat?*
Someone: *You said: "Let's cross over to the other side."*
Jesus: *Did I say we would perish along the way?*
Someone: *No sir, you said: "Let's cross over to the other side."*
Jesus: *Ok, that's what we are doing. Wake me up when we get there.*

But that's not what He did. This is what He did…

³⁹ *Then He arose and rebuked the wind, and said to the sea, "Peace be still!" And the wind ceased and there was a great calm.* ⁴⁰ *But He said to them, "Why are you so fearful? How is it that you have no faith?"* ⁴¹ *And they feared exceedingly, and said to one another, "Who can this be, that even the wind and the sea obey Him!"*

When He said: *Peace be still!* – everything was peaceful and still. The storm was gone. It wasn't just calm, but there was a great calm. Then He addressed their fear. He asked why they were so fearful. Obviously, He had told them they were going over to the other side. Storms happen. But they were going to the other side.

What's odd was their response. When he followed up by asking how it was that they had no faith, they feared exceedingly. Why are we all so fearful at times? Why is it that we don't seem to have faith?

There is a certain peace that only Jesus can give. All we have to do is ask for it and receive it. He promised. We can know peace by knowing Him.

REFLECTION QUESTIONS

1. Would you say your life is peaceful? If not, why?

2. What do you believe is different about the peace Jesus gives vs what the world may give?

3. Journal your thoughts after reading Mark 4:35-38.

4. Had you been on the boat that day, what would you have felt? How would you have responded to the question Jesus asked in Mark 4:40? Why are you so fearful?

5. What is your prayer concerning this chapter?

GAME 9:

Believe

¹⁶ For God so loved the world that He gave His only begotten Son, that whoever believes in Him should not perish but have everlasting life.

JOHN 3:16 (NKJV)

²³ Jesus said to him, "If you can believe, all things are possible to him who believes."

MARK 9:23

⁶ But without faith it is impossible to please Him, for he who comes to God must believe that He is, and that He is a rewarder of those who diligently seek Him.

HEBREWS 11:6

⁵ If any of you lacks wisdom, let him ask of God, who gives to all liberally and without reproach, and it will be given to him. ⁶ But let him ask in faith, with no doubting, for he who doubts is like a wave of the sea driven and tossed by the wind.

JAMES 1:5-6

What you believe can change everything. Each of us has a belief window through which we see the world around us. It includes what we believe about ourselves, what we believe about others, and what we believe about everything else in life, including what we believe about God.

Our belief windows can be correct, or we can believe things in error. So, as you can see, what you believe is vastly important to everything concerning our lives. Ken Blanchard and Hyrum Smith have written and said much about Belief Windows. In an article written by Ken Blanchard titled, *What Principles Are On Your Belief Window*, he said…

> On our belief window are thousands of principles we believe to be true about ourselves, our world, and other people. Most of these principles are an attempt to meet a basic human need such as to live, to love and be loved, to feel important, or to have variety. Some principles, such as "the Earth is round," reflect reality, and some, such as "dogs are better than cats," are subjective. Either way, we believe them to be true and we will behave as if they are—because our beliefs drive our behavior.

We are constantly verifying and questioning everything we see through our belief window. If the results of what we believe are giving us what we believe we need, we keep those principles in our belief window. If not, we find a new principle to believe. Now, think about that statement. Even what we allow to stay in view through our belief window is dependent on what we believe we need and whether we believe our beliefs are giving us the results we believe we need. You see, everything hinges on belief.

There is a made-up story told (author unknown) of a rock climber who was climbing in freezing temperature in complete darkness at night. Of course, we could discuss the validity of a belief that one should be climbing in complete darkness. Maybe the belief that the climb could be made was stronger than the belief that it wasn't a good idea climbing in complete darkness. Maybe the climber believed that overcoming the challenge was greater than the danger. Maybe the climber just started climbing too late in the evening. Either way, the climber slipped and fell.

At a point during the fall, the climber was saved by the safety harness and rope that he had worn for the climb. The moon and stars were covered by clouds and there was no visibility. It was getting colder and colder. The climber wasn't sure how far he had fallen or exactly how high he was when he slipped.

Dangling in his safety harness held by the rope and injured by the fall, the climber had no ability to pull himself up by the rope. In desperation, and in belief that God could help, he screamed out.

Climber: *God help me!*
He believed he heard God speak to him.

God: *What do you want me to do?*
As the story goes, the man said:

Climber: *Save me.*

God: *Do you believe I can save you?*

Climber: *Of course, I believe you can save me… you are God!*

God: *Then, according to your faith, cut the rope.*

There was a moment of silence as the man grasped the rope tighter and pondered what he believed he had heard from God.

At daylight, a rescue team was sent to find the climber after his family reported him missing.

When the rescue team found the man, he was frozen to death still in his safety harness, dangling two feet from the ground. Sometimes we must believe when we can't see. That's called faith.

In a boat, during a storm, the disciples saw a person walking on the water. They believed it might be a ghost. Obviously, everyone was afraid. But it wasn't a ghost. It was Jesus Himself. He spoke to them and said: *Be of good cheer! It is I; do not be afraid.* – Matthew 14:27(b) (NKJV)

Can you imagine what might be going through their belief windows?

At first, they thought it was a ghost. That's the only explanation in their collective belief window. People can't walk on water. Yet, it was Jesus! It was time to correct a faulty belief window principle. Jesus can walk on water!

Then Peter did something in direct conflict with his previous belief window principle concerning a person's ability to walk on water. He asked Jesus to invite (the NKJV word is translated as "command") him to come to where he was walking on the water.

Jesus did, and Peter got out of the boat and walked on water to Him.

Think about what was going on inside Peter's belief window at the time. He was walking on water. Not only was he walking on water, but the wind was blowing, and the sea was rough. Peter knew he was doing something he didn't think was possible only moments ago. What wasn't possible according to his belief window was happening. Yet… he also saw that the sea was rough. The old belief window principle concerning a person walking on water started to kick back in. He was afraid, even though Jesus had just told them not to be afraid. When that happened, he began to sink.

Like the climber in the rope story, he said: *Lord save me!* Matthew 14:30 (NKJV)

Like the climber in the rope story was saved by his safety harness and rope, Jesus reached out His hand and caught Peter and saved him. The difference is that now Peter wasn't holding on to a temporary rope protecting himself from perceived danger. Peter was holding on to The King of Kings and Lord of Lords.

Jesus asked Peter why he doubted. Even after having faith to get out of the boat and doing something no one other than Jesus had ever done, Peter let doubt slip in and he was afraid.

You see, just because we have faith, and believe the right things, we still must battle doubt at times. It's just a fact of life. That's why it's called the walk of faith. It's something we do daily, hourly, and even moment by moment.

James 1:5-6 (NKJV) teaches us that *he who doubts is like a wave of the sea driven and tossed by the wind.* There is a difference in believing what is true and being driven and tossed by the wind by having untrue beliefs in our belief window.

Reflection Questions

1. Most people can quote John 3:16. In your own words, what does it mean to you? What does it mean to believe in Jesus? How would you explain that verse to another person?

2. What does James 1:6 say about doubt?

3. How can you develop stronger belief windows concerning what God's word says about you?

4. What is your prayer concerning this chapter?

GAME 10:

Always Growing

When I was a child, I spoke as a child, I understood as a child, I thought as a child; but when I became a man, I put away childish things.
1 Corinthians 13:11 (NKJV)

Therefore, leaving the discussion of the elementary principles of Christ, let us go on to perfection, not laying again the foundation of repentance from dead works and of faith toward God...
Hebrews 6:1 (NKJV)

[12] For though by this time you ought to be teachers, you need someone to teach you again the first principles of the oracles of God; and you have come to need milk and not solid food. [13] For everyone who partakes only of milk is unskilled in the word of righteousness, for he is a babe. [14] But solid food belongs to those who are of full age, that is, those who by reason of use have their senses exercised to discern both good and evil.
Hebrews 5:12-14

God did not call us to sit still. We are called to grow, and to always be growing. To do that requires us to put away childish things. When we were a child, we were expected to speak as a child. When a child begins to make noises, most of those noises are not words. In fact, none of it is words. It's gibberish, but no one is concerned. That is, until a certain time. While the gibberish is natural for a while, it's not normal to remain in that state. After a while, the child begins to form words and then more words. At a point the child begins to speak in sentences. While that's normal, it's not yet the same as an adult speaking.

At that point, the child understands as a child understands, and thinks as a child thinks. So, when the child says childish things, there is no concern. Yet, as the child becomes older, the understanding and thinking process has grown and is reflected in what is said. If that doesn't happen, there is concern. But there is more. Hebrews 6:1 instructs us to *go on to perfection*. We leave the *discussion of the elementary principles of Christ.* We are instructed to become mature Christ followers. That means mastery. That takes work and the work is fruitful.

While the growth of a child is natural, there must be good nutrition involved. The same applies to spiritual growth. Obviously, at first, a baby is consuming milk or baby formula. Nobody feeds a baby steak. But the nutrition the baby needs is in the milk or formula. However, as the baby grows into a toddler, the baby begins to eat solid food… still not steak, but solid food. Think about the last part of Hebrews 5:14 (NKJV)… *those who by reason of use have their senses exercised to discern both good and evil.*

In terms of spiritual growth, just as with our physical body, we need basic nutrition with the span of that nutrition growing along with exercise. We are to exercise our faith for it to grow. Just as muscles grow because of resistance type exercises, our faith grows as we exercise and practice it in our daily lives.

What is the alternative? If we aren't growing, we become stagnant in our faith. Just as a child without a growing vocabulary will be come stagnant in their ability to communicate, our faith is the same. So, if we aren't growing, we become weaker.

In medical terms, inactivity of a person's muscles brings on what is called muscle atrophy. That simply means that, without active use, the body will naturally break the muscle down to conserve energy. One study suggests that without use, within ten days a person could lose 11% of a muscle that is not used. Remember, scripture (Psalm 139:14 – NKJV) says *I am fearfully and wonderfully made*. Our bodies are complex, yet very efficient. If you don't use it, you will lose it. Our walk of faith works the same way. We should always be growing.

Consider the parable of the talents. (Matthew 25:14-30)

In this parable, a man was about to go on a journey and called his servants together. To each, he gave a certain number of talents according to their ability. Today, we think of talents as skills… the ability to play a sport, or an instrument, or sing, etc. In that day, a talent represented a unit of money. Biblical scholars differ in what they believe to be the value of a talent. Some believe it to be worth twenty years of wages. That's a big number no matter what you might make in a year!

To one, he gave five talents, to another he gave two, and to the third one he gave one. It's important to consider that to each he gave according to his own ability. Think about it. There was a reason for that decision. He didn't give more than the person had the ability to handle. Therefore, there must have been an expectation.

Then he left on his journey.

The one who had five talents traded with them (somehow invested them) and had in return five more talents. The one who was given two talents gained two more. They each grew what they had been given. It's interesting that, as he gave according to the ability of each, the one with five talents gained five more and the one with two talents gained two more. It seems like he understood their ability. But what about the one with one talent?

In terms of ability, you would expect the one with one talent to gain one more and have two. However, that wasn't the case. Rather than using his ability, he buried his talent and did nothing with it. Oh, he had an excuse. He said he didn't want to lose it. That means he didn't grow it. Do you see where this story is going?

He obviously had the ability to grow one talent. No one expected him to manage growing five talents or two talents. That's not what was given to him. It was one talent.

After an extended period, the man returned and settled accounts with the ones to whom he had given the talents. It went well for the one who had been given five and had gained five more, as well as the one to whom two talents had been given and two more gained. To them, it was said:

...Well done, good and faithful servant; you have been faithful
over a few things, I will make you ruler over many things.
Enter into the joy of your lord.
MATTHEW 25:23 (NKJV)

But not so for the one who was given one talent and had not grown it. To the one who had not grown in talents because his one was buried, it was said:

...You wicked and lazy servant, you knew that I reap where I
have not sown, and gather where I have not scattered seed.
So you ought to have deposited my money with the bankers,
and at my coming I would have received back my own with
interest. So take the talent from him, and give it to him who
has ten talents.
MATTHEW 25:26-28

This parable is about always growing and the great peril of not
growing.

Go grow! Always be growing!

Reflection Questions

1. In what area of your life do you feel stagnant or stuck? What can you do to change that status?

2. What do you believe you would have done had you been a participant in the parable of talents?

3. What do you believe the words ...*faithful over a few things*... mean in Matthew 25:23?

4. In what areas do you need to grow? What are the next steps you will take? By when?

5. What is your prayer concerning this chapter?

GAME 11:

Press Forward

I have been crucified with Christ; it is no longer I who live, but Christ lives in me; and the life which I now live in the flesh I live by faith in the Son of God, who loved me and gave Himself for me.

GALATIANS 2:20 (NKJV)

Therefore, if anyone is in Christ, he is a new creation; old things have passed away; behold, all things have become new.

2 CORINTHIANS 5:17

[12] Not that I have already attained, or am already perfected; but I press on, that I may lay hold of that for which Christ Jesus has also laid hold of me. [13] Brethren, I do not count myself to have [b]apprehended; but one thing I do, forgetting those things which are behind and reaching forward to those things which are ahead, [14] I press toward the goal for the prize of the upward call of God in Christ Jesus.

PHILIPPIANS 3:12-14

In football, the focus of the offense is to press forward, moving the chain, and reaching the goal line to score. Obviously, the defense is focused on preventing any forward movement of the ball. In life, we have an enemy that is always trying to prevent us from moving forward.

There are also times in life when we are playing defense and it feels like the enemy is trying to take our ground and score on us. In either case, we have to press forward toward what is in front of us whether it be moving forward or running forward into battle to defend our territory. There are also times when we aren't facing the enemy, but rather the battle is against our own selves. Even then, we still have to press forward.

Consider this story about a friend named Adam. During his freshman year he was not part of his high school football team. He and his dad attended the final game of the year and witnessed Adam's high school team being decimated by their cross-town rival.

As they were leaving the stadium, Adam made a statement to his dad.

Adam: *I don't like what just happened, Dad.*

Adam's Dad: *You mean in the game?*

Adam: *Yeah, I don't like the way they beat us… especially with it being them.*

Adam's Dad: *Well, you can do something about it.*

Adam: *What can I do? The game is over.*

Adam's Dad: *True. But you can join the team and help them win next year's game.*

Two days later, Adam told his dad he had joined the football team. The next year, during a junior varsity game, Adam was playing the position of linebacker. During one play, he broke through the line and the only thing between Adam and the quarterback was green grass. The quarterback had his back to Adam and was looking for a receiver down field. He didn't see Adam coming. Adam was closing the distance between himself and the quarterback and his dad was holding on tight to his binoculars just waiting for Adam to sack the quarterback.

However, although Adam was running, he wasn't getting anywhere fast. At the last moment, the quarterback caught a glimpse of Adam barreling down on him and just threw the ball out of bounds. Adam didn't even get to hit him. The play was over, and the game went on.

After the game, Adam's dad asked what happened during that play. He told Adam that he saw he had a clear shot at the quarterback, but that it seemed to take him too long to get there. Adam looked at his dad and said: *You saw that, didn't you?* His dad nodded and asked Adam what happened. Adam told his dad that it seemed like he had imaginary blockers between him and the quarterback. Of course, he told his dad that he didn't really see anyone, but that something seemed to be slowing him down.

Adam's dad assured him that what had just happened to him was perfectly normal. At first, Adam didn't understand. But his dad asked him if he had felt like he was trying to run in a swimming pool in chest deep water. Surprised at the question which accurately described what he was feeling, Adam asked his dad how he knew.

His dad told him that we have all been in situations like that before. He explained to Adam that although he knew it was his job to hit the quarterback, it was his first time to really get to hit someone on the other team. This was different than practice. Adam realized that there was a lot going on in his head during that part of the play. He had wondered things like, should he hit him high or low, how hard should he hit him, and should he also try to knock the ball out of his hands. So many questions were racing through his mind that it really did slow him down.

The imaginary blockers weren't real, but the thoughts going through Adam's mind during the play disrupted his ability to... well, make the play. What was going on in his mind really did slow him down and prevented him from pressing forward to do what he knew it was his role to do.

We all face things like that in life whether it be lack of confidence, naysayers, past experiences, and the list goes on. But in football, and life, we must find a way to press forward.

As in Galatians 2:20, we must take the focus off us and place it on Christ. *It is no longer I who live, but Christ lives in me.* When my focus is less on me and more on Christ who lives in me, the imaginary blockers fade away.

I must realize and consider that my past failures and mistakes are a thing of the past. It is important to realize that, as 2 Corinthians 5:17 (NKJV) states, I am a new creation in Christ... *old things have passed away; behold, all things have become new.* I am not the sum of my failures; I am a new creation.

Although I haven't made it yet, I know I need to forget what is behind. The only thing I can do about the past is learn from it. The only thing I can do about the future is plan for it. The only day I can act and do anything about is today.

Today, I can and should reach forward to those things that are ahead. Today I can and should press forward *toward the goal for the prize of the upward call of God in Christ Jesus.*

Reflection Questions

1. In your own words, what do you believe the words ... is a new creation; old things have passed away; behold, all things have become new... mean in 2 Corinthians 5:17?

2. What does Paul mean by ...*I press on*... in Philippians 3:12? ...and later in Philippians 3:14 when he said: *I press toward the goal for the prize of the upward call of God in Christ Jesus...* - what exactly do you believe he is pressing toward?

3. Do you believe you are facing imaginary blockers in any area of your life? What do you believe you should do to overcome those imaginary blockers?

4. What is your prayer concerning this chapter?

GAME 12:

Grateful

...in everything give thanks; for this is the will of
God in Christ Jesus for you.
1 THESSALONIANS 5:18 (NKJV)

Jesus Christ is the same yesterday, today, and forever.
HEBREWS 13:8 (NKJV)

God's word teaches us to give thanks in everything. It says this is the will of God in Christ Jesus for us. It is so important to give thanks. It's also easy to forget to give thanks. That doesn't mean that forgetting to give thanks is being ungrateful. It just means that, as humans, it's easy to forget.

In Luke 17, we find Jesus on His way to Jerusalem. As He went on His way, he passed through Samaria and Galilee. As He was entering a village along the way, He met ten lepers standing off to the side. They noticed that it was Jesus and yelled out to him... *Jesus, Master, have mercy on us!*

When Jesus saw them, he said to them to go and show themselves to the priests. Scripture says that as they went, they were cleansed. Think about that... as they went, they were cleansed.

Can you imagine how they felt when they realized they were completely healed. No more leprosy. It was gone! How grateful would you be?

Leprosy is a horrible disease. It's also visible. Everybody knew these 10 men had it. People who had it were even labeled with the name... they were known as lepers. They had to live outside of the city. It was a horrible life to live. Yet, these 10 were completely healed. After they showed themselves to the priests, they could go back to their normal lives. They had just been given one of the most incredible gifts imaginable. But only one came back to thank Jesus.

I would like to think I would have been the one to go back and thank Jesus. Would you?

We all get busy and forget to be grateful at times. Let this be the day you are grateful. In fact, let every day for the rest of your life be days you are grateful. If you know Jesus as your personal Savior, thank Him. He has cleansed you from something more dreadful than leprosy. If you don't know Him as your personal Savior, I invite you to do that today. Then be grateful for Him for saving you.

Of course, I am using the words grateful and thankful interchangeably. I am suggesting that you have a heart of appreciation and that you share that with others. Let them know.

So, that's what I am going to do here. Of the multitude of people that I want to thank and show gratitude, here are a few...

We are grateful to you for picking up this book and reading it. Tim and I invested countless hours putting this book together for you because we believe in the power of the story that God has allowed me to live, and in the power of His word through the 12 Games of chapels that I shared with the team at the University of Mississippi during the 2022 football season. It is our hope that

God uses the words He gave us to write this book to impact your life in a positive way. We hope that you will want to use this book to impact others by giving them a copy of it and sharing your story with them. Your story is important, too!

SAMMIE'S GRATITUDE...

There are so many I owe a debt of gratitude to, but none more impactful than Jesus Christ. Thank You Lord for always protecting me, walking with me, encouraging me, and never giving up on me when I deserved much less. Thank you to all the coaches, teammates, and support staff with whom I have been blessed with the opportunity to compete, to mentor, and be mentored by. Thank you to all the seen and unseen family and friends that have prayed for me during great times as well as difficult times. Thank you to all the Ministry partners that have and continue to give of their time, talents and treasure that make it possible for me to share the Gospel and the impact that surrendering and accepting Jesus as my Savior has had on my life. Thanks to all the friends and colleagues that have endorsed my book. Thank you, Joan Enochs, for all the love and behind the scenes work on this book, as well as lending me your son to see this project through. Thank you, Tim Enochs, for encouraging me to share my story with others who may have never had the opportunity to hear it. I believe God always connects the dots and puts people in our lives for His glory. I firmly believe He's glorified in our friendship and passion for seeing lives changed. Thank you, Mom & Dad, for being the example of love, guidance, and encouragement that I pray I'm exhibiting to my children, grandchildren and all whom God has placed in my sphere of influence. Last, but certainly not the least, thank you to my beautiful wife, Shalonda. You have been my rock and inspirational supporter, and you're all I envisioned as a lifelong partner.

I know I can count on you for help, prayer, a shoulder to cry on, and to be the model of a woman who loves Jesus. I thank God for allowing me to be a man that found a wife and a good thing.

TIM'S GRATITUDE...

Like Sammie, there are so many I owe a debt of gratitude to, and none more so than Jesus Christ, my Lord and Savior. I am so thankful for your mercy and grace, and for the opportunity to get to do what You have called me to do. Thank you to my family and friends who have given encouragement and understanding while working on this project. Special thanks to Mom who has done a lot of work behind the scenes to make this project better. God has seen what you have done, and you will be rewarded for it. Thank you, Sammie, for allowing me to work on this project with you. In all the interviews, etc. that I got to do with your friends and family, I have never seen someone so loved and appreciated as you, brother. God is using you and will continue to use you in a special way that has great impact on other people. Thanks to the people who will read this book. Thank you for trusting us with your valuable time as you read through the pages. May what you have read encourage you and have a positive impact on your life. Always remember, Sammie's name is Sammie, not 18121-018, the number given to him by the Federal Bureau of Prisons (FBOP).

There is a reason that S. Truett Cathy, Founder of Chick-fil-A, claimed Proverbs 22:1 as his life verse. There is a reason Sammie doesn't answer to 18121-018 anymore, and there is a reason for you to consider the value of your name and that your good name is to be chosen rather than great riches and loving favor rather than silver and gold.

A good name is to be chosen rather than great riches,
Loving favor rather than silver and gold.

PROVERBS 22:1

REFLECTION QUESTIONS

1. Make a list for all things for which you are thankful. Take time to pray and give God thanks for these blessings He has given you in life.

2. Make a list of the people in your life who you should thank for what they have done to help you become the person you are.

3. Use your list as a checklist and begin to thank each person either personally or by a personal handwritten note being specific for why you are thankful to each one. If a person on your list has already passed away, find someone in their family or one of their friends and share why you are thankful to that person.

4. What is your prayer concerning this chapter?

ABOUT THE AUTHOR:

SAMMIE SMITH

Sammie Smith is a former NFL first round draft pick and Florida State University football hall of fame inductee. Sammie has overcome challenges in his personal and professional life by surrendering his life to Jesus Christ. Sammie lives in Mount Dora, Florida with his wife Shalonda, they both serve others through the Fellowship of Christian Athletes, they have three children, daughter Jenee' (married to Wallace Taylor) Son Cre'shawn, daughter Sania. Three grandchildren, Christian, Cam, and Hazel Grace.

TIM ENOCHS

Tim has been a successful Executive Coach for over 21 years and has more than 12,000 hours of one-on-one coaching time. He is a New York Times Bestselling Author, Film Producer, and speaker. He has written and co-authored multiple books including Every Day is Game Day, Uncommon Influence, 49 Days Back to Better, The Foundation, The Street

Sweeper and The CHILD Game Plan. His book, On The Clock, made it to #12 on the New York Times Bestsellers List. Tim is also the Executive Producer for the movie Welcome to Inspiration based on his book, The Street Sweeper. He is currently working on a movie inspired by On The Clock. Tim is the Senior Executive Coach and Co-Founder of NEWLife Leadership and Irrefutable Success University. His passion is helping people discover their purpose, set big goals and achieve those goals.

IRREFUTABLE
SUCCESS
UNIVERSITY

FIRST MONTH FREE!!!

DISCOVER YOUR PURPOSE IN LIFE

MAKE YOUR VISION CLEAR

CREATE A MASTER PLAN

EXPERIENCE IRREFUTABLE SUCCESS IN LIFE AND WORK

A free ebook edition is available with the purchase of this book.

To claim your free ebook edition:

1. Visit MorganJamesBOGO.com
2. Sign your name CLEARLY in the space
3. Complete the form and submit a photo of the entire copyright page
4. You or your friend can download the ebook to your preferred device

Print & Digital Together Forever.

Snap a photo

Free ebook

Read anywhere